WILLIS RICHARDSON, FORGOTTEN PIONEER OF AFRICAN-AMERICAN DRAMA

Willis Richardson (1889–1977). Photo courtesy of Christine Rauchfuss Gray.

WILLIS RICHARDSON, FORGOTTEN PIONEER OF AFRICAN–AMERICAN DRAMA

❖

Christine Rauchfuss Gray
Foreword by Bernard L. Peterson, Jr.

Contributions in Afro-American and African Studies,
Number 190

GREENWOOD PRESS
Westport, Connecticut • London

Library of Congress Cataloging-in-Publication Data

Gray, Christine Rauchfuss.
    Willis Richardson, forgotten pioneer of African-American drama /
Christine Rauchfuss Gray ; foreword by Bernard L. Peterson, Jr.
        p.   cm.—(Contributions in Afro-American and African
studies, ISSN 0069-9624 ; no. 190)
    Includes bibliographical references and index.
    ISBN 0-313-30373-8 (alk. paper)
    1. Richardson, Willis, 1889-   .   2. Dramatists, American—20th
century—Biography.   3. Afro-American dramatists—Biography.
4. Afro-Americans in literature.   I. Title.   II. Series.
PS3535.I3374Z68   1999
812'.52
[B]—dc21   98-15597

British Library Cataloguing in Publication Data is available.

Library of Congress Catalog Card Number: 98-15597
ISBN: 0-313-30373-8
ISSN: 0069-9624

First published in 1999

Greenwood Press, 88 Post Road West, Westport, CT 06881
An imprint of Greenwood Publishing Group, Inc.
www.greenwood.com

Printed in the United States of America

The paper used in this book complies with the
Permanent Paper Standard issued by the National
Information Standards Organization (Z39.48-1984).

10 9 8 7 6 5 4 3

Copyright Acknowledgment

The author and publisher gratefully acknowledge permission to reprint the following material:

Excerpts from Willis Richardson's recorded interview with Larry Galvin. Reprinted
with permission from Hatch-Billops Collection, Inc.

Contents

❖

Foreword

In 1975, just before the American Bicentennial celebration, I published a fairly long article on Willis Richardson,[1] in which I attempted to call attention to his significance as a pioneer in the development of African-American drama. In that article I expressed my concern that he had not received the attention that he deserved and my hope that interest in his work would soon be revived. I have been somewhat gratified, in the intervening years, to discover that an increasing number of studies have included substantial sections on Richardson's plays, but to my great disappointment these added little to the information that I myself had been able to unearth through preliminary investigation. Christine Gray's contribution of the first full-length study of Richardson's life and work will undoubtedly help, at last, to stimulate new interest in this important pioneer playwright. Through her discovery of hitherto-unpublished and relatively unexamined autobiographical materials, her interviews of Richardson's family, and her examination of taped interviews of Richardson himself, she has put into place the importance of this early African-American dramatist. As a result of her research on and her critical analysis of Richardson's published and unpublished plays, Gray has cast new light on Richardson, both the man and his work.

As a genuine theatrical pioneer who was, indeed, the first critically significant and productive African-American playwright,
Richardson forged the way for countless others who came after
him, many of whom were able to garner the laurels and accolades
that he himself was not accorded during his lifetime, much to his
frustration and disappointment. For he was well aware that his pioneering accomplishments were numerous and deserving of recognition and acknowledgment. Christine Gray has undertaken the
task of recovering and acknowledging Richardson's life and
achievements in this volume.

Having written forty-eight individual plays, Richardson was one
of the most prolific playwrights of his time. Despite his vast output,
Richardson is still best remembered for what should have only been a
footnote in the history of African-American drama—the fact that he
was the first black playwright to have a serious play produced on
Broadway. This event, the opening of *The Chip Woman's Fortune* in
1923, achieved its historical significance because of the tendency, then
and now, to evaluate achievements of African Americans by their success within the white community.

The Broadway production of the three plays performed in 1923
by the Ethiopian Art Players of Chicago (also called the Chicago
Folk Theatre), in which Richardson's one-act folk drama, *The Chip
Woman's Fortune*, was showcased, was backed by two prominent
white theatrical personalities—Tennessee Anderson, married to
the Chicago novelist and author, Sherwood Anderson, was a spon-
sor, and Raymond O'Neil, founder and former artistic director of
the Cleveland Play House, was director. Prior to making its stage
debut, the all-black cast trained intensively for a year under the
joint tutelage of O'Neil and the All-American Theatre Association,
one of Chicago's white theatrical schools and playhouses. With
such prestigious patronage, it was inevitable that this project
would have a memorable impact on white critics. They immediately lauded the Broadway production as a *succes d'estime*, or (more
properly) a triumph of "white" artistic achievement. For the black
cast, however, this enterprise ended more in disappointment than
in triumph, because O'Neil, the director, "absconded with the proceeds" of the Broadway production, leaving the players stranded.
Although numerous earlier black minstrel and vaudeville troupes
had been abandoned in this manner by unscrupulous white man-

agers, this was a wholly unexpected turn of events after a twentieth-century Broadway success, especially in view of O'Neil's prestige as a director.

As Gray points out, Richardson "was at one time considered the hope and promise of black drama, a playwright whose work was in great demand by little theater groups and drama clubs...." He was the first African-American playwright to provide a significant body of plays for production by amateur theatre groups, including the Howard Players of Washington, D.C., the Gilpin Players of Cleveland, the Dunbar Dramatic Club of Harlem, the Hampton Players of Virginia, the Krigwa Players of New York City and Washington, D.C., and the Dixwell Players of New Haven, Connecticut.[2] Richardson's plays were produced more frequently by black high school, college, and community groups than were those by any other African-American playwright. Richardson lamented that he was rarely paid or even asked permission for these productions.

As Gray tells us, when Richardson first tried to get his plays produced at Howard University, Stanley Durkee, the president of the institution, flatly refused, only later granting permission after Richardson's reputation had been established by the Broadway production. Except for plays written by Howard's own students, in the playwriting classes of Montgomery Gregory, Richardson's one-act domestic drama *Mortgaged* was the first black-authored play to be staged by the Howard Players—on March 29, 1924. Similarly, his folk drama *Compromise* was the first play by a black author to be presented by the Gilpin Players at the Karamu Theatre in Cleveland—on February 25, 1925.

Gray provides us with much new material on Richardson's life, which helps in understanding the man behind the plays. Although she admits that numerous gaps in her biographical account may never be filled, hers is the closest to a full biography of Richardson that we have ever had. Her book reveals many of the complexities of his persona that had hitherto eluded previous researchers, including myself. From Gray's biographical account, we learn the details of Richardson's education and employment, and the notable people who influenced his life and work. Of these, the most influential were, perhaps, W.E.B. Du Bois and Alain Locke. Gray also reveals the political troubles that Richardson faced as a government employee because of "suspected left-wing sympathies," including his relationship with Du Bois. She notes the tragedy of his daughter's death and his puzzlement over the portrayal of African-American life in the dramas of the civil-rights struggle, which made his plays by comparison obsolete. According to Gray, Richardson's final years were plagued by disappointment, failing health, physical dependence, loneliness, and (above all) lack of recognition.

As a necessary background for understanding Richardson's plays, Gray discusses the development of African-American drama in the early twentieth. She holds that because scholarly attention often focuses on the Harlem Renaissance, the significance and importance of literary activities in other areas, including Washington, D.C., where Richardson lived and worked, are often overlooked. She notes that the development of black drama was greatly influenced by white writers—most notably Ridgely Torrence, Paul Green, and Eugene O'Neill—who achieved their early success writing plays of Negro life. These writers, in focusing primarily on the exotic and primitive elements that they saw in black culture, were not particularly interested in accurate portrayals of African-American life. Because many black professional writers in Harlem sought to gain the favor and financial support of white patrons, philanthropists, producers, and publishers, who were interested in encouraging and developing African-American talent, they too were compelled to explore and exploit the more primitive, exotic, and sensational aspects of their own black culture, which whites found so fascinating. In his 1929 Broadway play *Harlem*, for example, Wallace Thurman portrayed Harlem as a wild, romantic, and exotic playground, and as a den of corruption and iniquity where such vices as gambling, prostitution, sexual promiscuity, racketeering, drinking, drugs, and murder were common occurrences. These exotic, primitive, and sensational elements were typical of the "Harlem style" of writing.

This catering to white tastes, however, was not incumbent upon black writers in other regions, who were free to explore commonplace and realistic aspects of black folk culture. Taking their cues from the manifestos of the Negro little theatre movement, spawned principally by the Drama Committee of the NAACP, Du Bois, and Alain Locke, these regional African-American playwrights dedicated themselves to more valid portrayals of blacks on stage and to the destruction of the old Negro stereotypes that had been perpetuated by white writers. These writers were free to tackle social issues and themes relevant to black culture such as poverty and unemployment, racism, lynching, slavery, patriotism, black migration, voting and women's rights, social striving of the black middle class, "passing," and miscegenation.

Added to the above themes was that of black history, which was vigorously promoted in the academic arena by Carter G. Woodson, an African-American historian who encouraged black playwrights to use the stage for teaching African Americans about the black contributions to civilization. Encouraged by Du Bois to stay within the black community, to write especially for it, and to direct their plays to black audiences, these regional writers were able to develop plays of Negro life that were more "authentic" and representative than those written by either white or black writers who were obliged to cater to white audiences in New York.

As Gray points out, the direction in which black drama should be developed was filled with controversy on the parts of its leading advocates, Du Bois and Locke. Du Bois was primarily interested in the use of the stage for propaganda in the fight against racism, while Locke was more concerned with the development of Negro folk drama as a serious art form. Both men were in agreement, however, that a native African-American drama should be developed and promoted.

In discussing Richardson's development as a playwright and his approach to drama, Gray details the influence of Du Bois, who considered education and uplifting of the African-American audiences to be the primary purpose of black drama. Gray finds that most of Richardson's plays differed from those by the majority of his contemporaries in avoiding themes that focused on tensions between the races and in shunning the more stirring conflicts of black life in favor of the mundane and ordinary problems faced by the average black person. In my own analysis of Richardson's plays, I find that his only play to sensationalize racial conflict is *Compromise*. Instead, most of his plots involve tensions within the black family and the community, tensions caused by petty jealousy and rivalry; greed, poverty, and the need for money to pay off debts; malicious gossip; treachery of family or group members; black-on-black exploitation; extravagant life styles; and other internal family and group conflicts.

Gray tells us that Richardson's family background, his rural upbringing, and his lack of both a college degree and social connections may have caused him to be especially sympathetic to the
problems of the black working class, and that in his folk dramas he
gave this class "a dignity not ordinarily accorded them." Richardson believed, according to Gray, that cultivated blacks were too
similar to white people to be typical of the African-American race.
He was, therefore, frequently critical of upper class, successful,
college-educated blacks who "ignore or abuse those who are
weaker financially or socially." In Gray's view, all of Richardson's
significant plays deal with the importance of the black community—the benefits of supporting it, and the consequences of denying this support. In his desire to educate black audiences, according
to Gray, Richardson tried to provide situations that would reveal
"the damage [that] blacks inflict on other blacks through their lack
of support." In his plays, he tried to show that a failure to respond
to the needs of the black community is detrimental not only to the
individual, the family, and the community, but also to the race as a
whole. Her examination of ten of Richardson's best-known plays
illustrates the importance of community support, whether it be
"emotional, financial, or spiritual." In her analysis, Gray interprets
community support as the help and encouragement that blacks
provide, or refuse to provide, in time of need to their family, friends,
neighbors, and others in the community. Most of his plays, according to Gray, focus on the denial of such support.

Gray provides an overview of other literary materials by Richardson, not previously discussed. These works include his history
plays, children's plays, unpublished and unproduced manuscripts, essays, short stories, and poetry.

Although Richardson's history plays are considered critically
less important than his folk plays, they were, when first published,
exceedingly popular among black teachers, students, and school
audiences. Gray discusses how Richardson's interest in writing,
compiling, and publishing black history plays was influenced and
encouraged by his association with Carter G. Woodson, cofounder
and editor of the *Journal of Negro History*, founder of the Association
for the Study of Negro Life and History, and head of the Associated
Publishers—all headquartered in Washington, D.C.

The dissemination of Richardson's black history plays was made possible by their inclusion in two anthologies edited by him and published by the Associated Publishers, under the sponsorship of Woodson and his Association for the Study of Negro Life and History. Gray provides pertinent information about the black history plays included in both of these anthologies, *Plays and Pageants from the Life of the Negro* (1930) and *Negro History in Thirteen Plays* (1935), the latter coedited with black playwright May Miller.[3]

In discussing Richardson's six essays on African-American drama, Gray calls attention to their significance in understanding his theory of Negro drama as an educational medium, and his plea for the writing of plays that reveal the soul of the Negro people. Gray considers Richardson's essays "the only body of theory on black drama" written by an African-American dramatist in the early twentieth century. His earliest essay, "The Hope of a Negro Drama," published in 1919, set forth the need and a formula for writing African-American plays. It preceded by several years the writings on black drama by both Du Bois and Locke.

Gray sums up her view on Richardson's contributions as an early black dramatist, and reiterates her regret that his plays, as well as those of other pioneer playwrights, have been greatly neglected. I, myself, was aware of this neglect when I published my second volume on African-American drama, titled *Early Black American Playwrights and Dramatic Writers* (1990). In my introduction, titled "The Origin and Development of the Black American Playwright from the Ante-bellum Period to World War II," I praised those early playwrights, among whom Richardson was prominently included, "for their courageous efforts to present truthful dramatizations of the lives and concerns of black people on the American stage, while also attempting to correct the distorted images and stereotypes that have too long been perpetuated by writers who lack a true knowledge of the black experience."

Christine Gray's concise, well-documented, and scholarly study of Richardson's life and work is significant in the field of American drama for it illuminates a corner in the history of the American stage that had hitherto been neglected. In doing so, it expands our understanding of American drama and of African-American literature. In recounting Richardson's achievements, Gray substanti-

ates the claim by several scholars that Willis Richardson, a pioneer playwright, is indeed "the father of African-American drama."

Bernard L. Peterson, Jr.

NOTES

1. "Willis Richardson: Pioneer Playwright," *Black World* 26, no. 6 (April 1975): 40–48, 86–88. Revised and republished in *The Theatre of Black Americans*, ed. Errol Hill (New York: Applause Books, 1987).

2. *Early Black American Playwrights and Dramatic Writers: A Biographical Directory and Catalog of Plays, Films, and Broadcasting Scripts*. Westport, CT: Greenwood Press, 1990. 21.

3. *Plays and Pageants* was reprinted in 1993 in a facsimile edition by the University Press of [Jackson] Mississippi, with an introduction by Christine Gray.

Chronology

❖

5 November 1889—Willis Richardson born in Wilmington, N.C.

18 April 1891—Mary Ellen Jones, his future wife, born in Washington, D.C.

1898—Richardson's parents buy house at the corner of Seventh and Taylor streets in Wilmington, N.C.

November 1898—Wilmington Riots

August 1899—Moves with his parents to Washington, D.C.

September 1899—Begins 7th grade at Cook School

October 1899—Transfers to the Slater School

1900—Attends Jones School

September 1906—Enters M Street School

1910?—Works for J. T. Jarvis in Washington, D.C., as a burnisher of pictures

17 June 1910—Graduates from M Street School

December 1910—Works for one month at the Library of Congress under Lee Phillips, Division of Maps and Charts

4 March 1911—Begins working at Bureau of Engraving and Printing as skilled helper in the wetting division at $2.11 per diem

1912—Meets his future wife, Mary Ellen Jones

14 September 1914—Marries Jones in Washington, D.C.

1915—Takes correspondence course in poetry from Cambridge Home Correspondence School in Springfield, Massachusetts. Receives a certificate from the school on 15 May 1916

1916—Begins correspondence course in drama

March 1916—With Otto Bohannan, sees Angelina Grimké's play *Rachel*

7 August 1916—Daughter Jean Paula born

29 April 1918—Daughter Shirley Antonella born

August 1918—Moves family to 2023 13th Street in Washington, D.C.

November 1919—*Crisis* publishes his essay "The Hope of a Negro Drama"

1920?—Richardson's mother dies

14 August 1920—Daughter Noel Justine born

November 1920—*The Deacon's Awakening*, his first play, published in *Crisis*

December 1920—*The King's Dilemma*, his first play for children, published in *The Brownies' Book*

1 January 1921—*The Deacon's Awakening* produced in St. Paul, Minn.

March 1921—*The Gypsy's Finger Ring* published in *The Brownies' Book*

June 1921—*The Children's Treasure* published in *The Brownies' Book*

October 1921—*The Dragon's Tooth* published in *The Brownies' Book*

1922—Is introduced to Langston Hughes in Carter G. Woodson's offices at Associated Publishers in Washington, D.C.; Wins the Washington, D.C., Public School Play Prize for *The King's Dilemma*; Receives a letter from Montgomery Gregory stating, "The sun is just beginning to shine on Negro art."

13 December 1922—Sends letter to Gregory stating "Negro drama has been, next to my wife and children, the very hope of my life. I shall do all within my power to advance it."

29 January 1923—*The Chip Woman's Fortune* produced in Chicago by Ethiopian Art Players

April 1923—Column runs in *Washington Star* on *The Chip Woman's Fortune*

30 April 1923—Ethiopian Art Players presents *The Chip Woman's Fortune* in Washington, D.C., at Howard University

15 May 1923—*The Chip Woman's Fortune* opens at the Frazee Theatre on Broadway, sharing the bill with Shakespeare's *The Comedy of Errors* and Wilde's *Salomé*

June 1923—*Crisis* publishes "The After Thought," an eight-line poem by Richardson

29 March 1924—*Mortgaged* produced by Howard Players of Howard University; aside from student productions, it is the first play by a black to be staged there

1924—Gregory leaves Howard University for a position as Superintendent of schools in Newark, N.J.; *Messenger* publishes Richardson's essay "Propaganda and the Stage"

October 1924—*Opportunity* publishes his essay "The Negro and the Stage"

1925—Alain Locke publishes *The New Negro*, which includes Richardson's play *Mortgaged*

April 1925—*Opportunity* publishes his essay "The Negro Audience"

20–22 May 1925—*Mortgaged* presented by Dunbar Dramatic Club at Plainfield Drama Tournament, N.J.

1 August 1925—*The Broken Banjo* presented in Washington, D.C.

9 August 1925—Locke receives letter thanking him for his changes to the ending of *Compromise*; Richardson encloses a capsule biography

12 August 1925—Receives telegram from Du Bois announcing his first prize in *Crisis* Drama Awards for *The Broken Banjo*; meets Arna Bontemps

Fall 1925—Meets Du Bois at *Crisis* Awards Banquet in New York City

September 1925—*Opportunity* publishes his essay "The Unpleasant Play"

1926—*Compromise* produced by Gilpin Players at Karamu House in Cleveland, Ohio; Wins *Crisis* Drama Award for *The Bootblack Lover*

1926–1935—Holds Krigwa gatherings and practices in his home; his wife is the group's secretary.

1926–1936—Meets weekly with Saturday Nighters at Georgia Douglas Johnson's home

3–17 May 1926— Produced by the Krigwa Players, *Compromise* and *The Broken Banjo* is presented with *The Church Fight*, by Ruth Gaines-Shelton, at the New York Public Library, in Harlem at 135th Street

21 May 1926—*The King's Dilemma* wins Public School Prize, Washington, D.C. (In his autobiography, Richardson listed this event as occurring in 1922)

1927—*The Flight of the Natives* published in Locke's *Plays of Negro Life*

3 February 1927—*Compromise* and *The House of Sham* produced by the Krigwa Players at Dunbar High School in Washington, D.C.

26 February 1927—*Compromise* and *The House of Sham* presented at Phillis Wheatley YWCA in Washington, D.C.

7 May 1927—*Mortgaged* and *Flight of the Natives* produced by Krigwa Players at Armstrong Auditorium under the auspices of the Cleveland Community Center

1928—Wins Edith Schwab Cup at Yale for *The Broken Banjo*; the play, produced by the Dixwell Players, competed against eight theater groups, all of them white

11 January 1928—*The Peacock's Feathers* produced by Krigwa Players in Washington, D.C.

11 February 1928—*Flight of the Natives* presented with *Blue Blood* by Georgia Johnson and *The Hunch* by Eulalie Spence at the Cleveland School in Washington, D.C.

23 March 1928—*House of Sham* presented by Paul Robeson Dramatic Club in Touglaloo, Miss.

6 December 1928—*The Nude Siren* and *The Chasm* (written with E. C. Williams) produced in Washington, D.C. by the Krigwa Players at Dunbar Community Center

1929—Drama Department at Howard University closes

15 February 1929—Morgan College, in Baltimore, produces *The House of Sham* at the Alhambra Theater in New York City with Paul Green's *The Man Who Died at 12 o'clock* and Randolph Edmonds' *Sirlock Bones*

April 1929—*The Idle Head* published in *Carolina Magazine*, the "drama edition"

9 May 1929?—The *House of Sham* and *The Broken Banjo* performed at the Alhambra Theater in New York City on bill with *Rackey* by Ernest Culbertson; the three plays go on tour to Wilkes-Barre, Penn., Roanoke, Va., and the Hampton Institute, Hampton, Va.

1930—For Carter Woodson, edits *Plays and Pageants from the Life of the Negro*; the collection includes Richardson's plays *The Black Horseman, The King's Dilemma, The House of Sham,* and *Attucks the Martyr*; Proposed as a candidate for Harmon Award in Literature

24 March 1930—*The Broken Banjo* and *House of Sham* presented at Hampton Institute

10 April 1930—*The House of Sham* in the One-Act Play Tournament at Garnett-Patterson Junior High School in Washington, D.C.; *The Chip Woman's Fortune* presented at Clark University, Atlanta

3 June 1930—*House of Sham* presented by Morehouse College Club in Atlanta

12 November 1930—*House of Sham* presented by the Brownsville High School in Brownsville, Tex.

6 February 1931—*Flight of the Natives* presented by the Coterie Club in Denver

11 March 1931—Receives letter from *UJSAG*, a newspaper in Budapest, asking permission to publish *Compromise*

19 March 1931—*House of Sham* presented at Maryland Normal School (now Bowie State College) in Bowie, Md.

5 April 1931—*UJSAG*, a Hungarian newspaper, publishes *Compromise*

23 April 1931—*House of Sham* presented at S. H. [?] High School in Merchantville, N.J.

29 April 1931—*House of Sham* presented by Virgin Islands Council in New York City

6 June 1931—*The Black Horseman* produced by Shaw High School Dramatic Club in Raleigh, N.C.

12 October 1931—*House of Sham, The Black Horseman,* and *The King's Dilemma* produced in Baltimore by the Playground Athletic League; *The*

Chip Woman's Fortune presented by Shaw University Players in Raleigh, N.C.

14 January 1932—*Mortgaged* and *The Chip Woman's Fortune* presented at Bishop College in Marshall, Tex.; *House of Sham* presented by Junior Book Lovers Club in Kansas City, Mo.

27 January 1932—*Compromise* produced by the Krigwa Players in Washington, D.C.

4 April 1932—*House of Sham* presented at Nanticoke High School in Nanticoke, Md.

12 April 1932—*Flight of the Natives* presented by the Gilpin Theater Guild in Birmingham, Ala.

18 April 1932—*House of Sham* presented at St. Augustine's College in Raleigh, N.C.

25 July 1932—*House of Sham* presented by East Mount Zion Church Club in Cleveland

28 September 1932—*House of Sham* presented at Townsend Community Center in Richmond, Ind.

1933—Listed in *Who's Who in Colored America*

5 January 1933—*House of Sham* presented at Lake City High School in Lake City, Fla.

23 January 1933—*House of Sham* presented by Calhoun School Players in Calhoun, Ala.

24 January 1933—*The King's Dilemma* presented at Morningside High School in Statesville, N.C.

13 February 1933—*House of Sham* presented in Louisville, Ky.

8 March 1933—*The Chip Woman's Fortune* presented by the Dramatic Club in Los Angeles

16 March 1933—*The Chip Woman's Fortune* presented at St. Phillips Junior College in San Antonio, Tex.

27 March 1933—*The Chip Woman's Fortune* presented at Florida A&M College, Gainesville

7 April 1933—*House of Sham* presented by First Methodist Episcopal Church, Mason City, Iowa

27 April 1933—*Mortgaged* presented at Florida A&M College, Gainesville

30 April 1933—*House of Sham* presented by YWCA Dramatic Club in New York City; *House of Sham* presented by Presbyterian Church Club in Rochester, N.Y.

5 November 1933—*House of Sham* presented at Orange County High School, Va.

11 December 1933—*House of Sham* presented in Belton?, S.C.

1934—*Attucks, the Martyr* presented by the Morgan College Players, Baltimore, Md.

9 February 1934—*Mortgaged* presented by Douglass High School Players, Baltimore, Md.; *Mortgaged* presented in Webster Groves, Mo.

1935—With May Miller, edits *Negro History in Thirteen Plays*; the collection includes Richardson's plays *Antonio Maceo*, *The Elder Dumas*, *In Menelik's Court*, and *Near Calvary*

11 February 1935—*The King's Dilemma* produced by Shaw Junior High School Players, Washington, D.C.

14 February 1935—For Negro History Week, *In Menelik's Court* produced at Morgan College by Morgan Players and at Douglass High School by Douglass High School Players, both schools located in Baltimore, Md.

15 February 1935—*In Menelik's Court* produced by Shaw Junior High School Players, Raleigh, N.C.

8 April 1936—*Compromise* presented in Washington, D.C. by the Howard Players

7 July 1936—Radio broadcast of *Mortgaged* on National Catholic Weekly

23 May 1937—Receives letter from Brother Bernardine in Uganda requesting a copy, "even second hand," of *Negro History in Thirteen Plays*

8 August 1937—Receives thank-you letter from Brother Bernardine in Uganda

28 April 1940—Receives letter from Montgomery Gregory calling Richardson a "pioneer playwright"

5 May 1941—*Miss or Mrs.* produced by the Bureau of Engraving Dramatic Club in Washington, D.C.

1942—Listed in *Who's Who in the East*?

22 July 1946—Swears in affidavit that he is not engaged in any strike against the federal government

1947—Admitted to the Author's League of America

7 March 1947—Daughter Noel commits suicide; Richardson and his wife take in her two daughters, Joyce and Noel Lois

11 September 1947—Fills out loyalty report for Bureau of Printing and Engraving; member of NAACP, AFL, Urban League

1950—Listed in *Who's Who in Colored America*

18 December 1951—Receives letter from Rowena Jelliffe thanking him for copies of plays and manuscripts he has sent to Karamu House

1952—Richardson and his wife adopt Noel's two daughters, Joyce and Noel Lois

31 March 1954—Retires from Bureau of Engraving and Printing

1956—*The King's Dilemma: Episodes of Hope and Dream,* a collection of his plays written for children, is published by Exposition Press; it includes *The King's Dilemma, The Dragon's Tooth, The Gypsy's Finger Ring, Near Calvary, The New Santa Claus,* and *Man of Magic*

5 December 1956—Letter from Langston Hughes thanking him for a copy of the book *The King's Dilemma*

1950s?—Approached by Leigh Whipper who wants to act as his agent in getting *The Amateur Prostitute* produced.

1960s—Corresponding secretary for the Derby Club

7 February 1960—*Attucks the Martyr* produced at Second Baptist Church in Long Branch, N.J., for Negro History Week

1964—Rewrites *Flight of the Natives* as a three-act play

1967—*Crisis* publishes short stories "He Holds His Head too High," "End of a Drop Out," and "Indian Summer Event"

5 February 1972—Receives letter from Drama Book Specialists saying the publisher is not interested in *The Amateur Prostitute*

2 March 1973—C. L. Harper High School produces *House of Sham*

12 March 1973—Joins the Harlem Arts Council

March 9, May 15, June 22, 1973—Receives three rejection letters from New York Shakespeare Festival for plays *The Amateur Prostitute, The Broken Banjo, The Visiting Lady* and *Joy Rider*

9–16 November 1973—Afro-American Studio in New York City produces *The Chip Woman's Fortune*

1974—Hospitalized in Belgrave Nursing Home, Silver Spring, Md.

13 June 1974—Letter from Hatch thanking Richardson for poem on the death of Duke Ellington; this is similar to the poem Richardson wrote on the death of Samuel Coleridge Taylor

1975—Appears on public television show in Trenton, N.J.

8 May 1976—Article "Who is Willis Richardson?" appears in *The Journal*, a black-owned newspaper in Wilmington, N.C.

7 November 1977—Dies in Washington, D.C.

21 November 1977—Receives AUDELCO Award as Outstanding Pioneer Playwright

Introduction

Plot 41971 in Lincoln Memorial Cemetery, roughly ten miles outside Washington, D.C., holds the remains of a man who was once considered a pioneer in the development of African-American drama. Now buried beside his wife and near his daughter Noel, Willis Richardson died quietly and in relative obscurity on 7 November 1977. Although during the 1920s and 1930s he was recognized as a significant black playwright and drama anthologist, Richardson was largely forgotten during the last four decades of his life. Crippled in the years before his death with Padgett's disease, the degeneration of cartilage, Richardson primarily involved himself with tending to his family and ill relatives, as his name faded even more from the fairly bright spotlight that had been his decades earlier. During his final years, few people were aware of his significant contributions to the development of African-American drama. Like his grave, Richardson's work is now largely unvisited.

In 1922, when he was 33 years old and establishing himself as a playwright, Richardson wrote to Montgomery Gregory, the head of the Drama Department at Howard University: "Negro drama . . . has been, next to my wife and children, the very hope of my life for several years. . . . I shall do all within my power to advance it." A survey of Richardson's achievements illustrates his commitment to this goal. During the 1920s and 1930s, his dramatic works were presented by numerous black high school, college, and university drama groups and by burgeoning little-theater groups in Chicago, New York, Washington, Cleveland, Baltimore, and Atlanta, as well as in cities and towns throughout the United States. Several of his fifty plays were published in *Crisis* and *Opportunity* magazines and in *The Brownies' Book*, a publication for children. In six essays published variously in *Crisis*, *Opportunity*, and *The Messenger*, Richardson urged black Americans to look to their own lives and circumstances for materials for the stage.[1] In addition, Richardson edited three anthologies of plays by African Americans: *Plays and Pageants from the Life of the Negro* (1930), the first published collection of plays containing works written only by African Americans; *Negro History in Thirteen Plays* (1935) with May Miller; and *The King's Dilemma: Episodes of Hope and Dream* (1956), a collection of his plays for children.

Between 1940 and his death in 1977, it became increasingly evident to Richardson that his plays were period pieces, works that reflected a time with different problems for blacks than the situations they faced between those dates. Changes in race relations after 1950 no doubt affected the public's taste for the type of plays that Richardson had written. Circumstances that his plays had explored in the black community had become less problematic; his plays seemed dated by 1955 when Rosa Park's refusal to give up her bus seat sparked the civil-rights movement of the next two decades. The changes wrought in American culture by *Brown v. the Board of Education*, incidents in Little Rock, lynchings in Mississippi, Martin Luther King's rise and assassination, and the message of Malcolm X—all were being reflected in plays by Alice Childress, Lorraine Hansberry, and playwrights of the Black Arts Movement of the 1960s and 1970s. These later African-American dramatists placed racial tensions at center stage, something Richardson's work had not done. Few of the developments on the black stage were of the sort Richardson had worked toward or expected. Although he had written his plays to educate blacks, his work now seemed to lack the passion, pulse, and charged messages heard in plays being written by Ed Bullins and Amiri Baraka.

In the years before his death, Richardson's plays had become the most important possessions in his life, for they represented his former acceptance and recognition by audiences and other artists in the 1920s and his pride in receiving such notice. Richardson's belief in his work, however unnoticed it may have been by the public, caused him in his final years to attempt vigorously, yet unsuccessfully, to preserve several of his plays through publication, if not production. His work rejected by publishers and producers, Richardson became embittered that he had not received the acknowledgment he had expected for his contributions to African-American drama. The man who was at one time considered the hope and promise of black drama, whose work had been in great demand by little-theater groups and drama clubs, who had committed much of his life to its development, died remembered by few others than his family and African-American theater historians, those who were aware of his earlier accomplishments.

Richardson and his works are not, however, alone in this regard. He is among many pioneers in black drama whose work has, unfortunately, received little attention. A remark made in 1988 by Richard Bernstein, theater columnist for the *New York Times*, must have made it obvious to theater historians and specialists in African-American drama that even more recent black stage history had been forgotten. In a column on August Wilson, Bernstein wrote, "The tradition of a black American theater is not a long one, going back only a generation or so to the work of such playwrights as Amiri Baraka" (32). Those who have studied African-American drama know the gross inaccuracy of this statement. Lorraine Hansberry's *A Raisin in the Sun*, which opened in 1959, roughly five years earlier than Baraka's plays, was acclaimed by white audiences and reviewers alike. Few audience members in 1959, or readers today, realize that in writing her best-known play, Hansberry was drawing on a tradition that was in place on the black stage since the early part of the century, a tradition that was itself rooted in African-American plays written in the nineteenth century.

Richardson and other black American dramatists of the 1920s defined, energized, and promoted the tradition of African-American drama by identifying the "voice" of authentic black American drama. As the pioneering playwrights of 1920s, Richardson and many others wrote their own versions of the plight of the

Younger family in Hansberry's play, of the racial tension in Baraka's *Dutchman*, of generational conflicts in August Wilson's
Fences. Richardson was instrumental in laying the foundation upon
which these and other African-American playwrights have built.
As the canon of American drama is re-evaluated, his contributions
to it are especially worth recovering and reviewing. Through his
plays and essays, readers can see the formulation and the creation
of an African-American voice in American drama.

Even in scholarly work discovering and recovering African-
American texts, the works of early black dramatists have generally
been neglected or dismissed in discussions of both American
drama and African-American literature. More than 360 non-
musical plays, however, were written by more than 140 African-
American playwrights before 1930. Indeed, much was obviously
going on in African-American drama during the early part of this
century, and much still waits to be located and explored.[2]

The recovery and acknowledgment of Willis Richardson's life
and work are the purpose of this book. Because of the neglect of so
much related to black drama during the 1920s, the focus of this
book must necessarily extend, to a degree, beyond this one playwright. In order to appreciate Richardson's significance, the reader
should examine his plays in the context of plays by his fellow black
dramatists. As will be evident, African-American drama is an ex-
tremely complex topic. Issues of audience, topic, and purpose are
compounded by the work of black writers in Harlem, by remnants
of the minstrel tradition, and by the encroachment of white playwrights seeking material on black folk culture for their own plays.
Unfortunately, few of these topics can be examined in depth for this
study. This book is limited to discussions related to the non-musical
stage and, except where necessary, materials on musicals and minstrelsy have been avoided. Many scholars have written extensively
on these topics.

The black dramatists discussed here were in several cases
prompted to write after seeing white interpretations of black life on
the stage and by the numerous stereotypes of blacks that littered
the white stages. Black playwrights had, in effect, two objectives:
one, to replace the mask of minstrelsy and white stereotypes with a
mirror that reflected, in many instances, the culture, anxieties, his-

tory, and plight of blacks in white America; the other, to develop and advance an authentic black voice for the stage.

Despite his efforts, Richardson's contributions have received minimal and uneven attention. For example, Doris Abramson's *Negro Playwrights in the American Theatre 1925–1959* (1969), long considered an important resource in the study of black dramatists, ignores Richardson completely, even though her often-cited book covers the period during which he was most active in drama. The scholars who mention Richardson do so only in a cursory manner, pointing most often to his play *The Chip Woman's Fortune* as the first non-musical play by an African American to appear on Broadway. Bernard Peterson's "Willis Richardson: Pioneer Playwright" is the only essay to concentrate solely on Richardson's significance as a playwright. Two other scholars treat Richardson's work in some detail. In *The Curtain and the Veil: Strategies in Black Drama* (1981), Helene Keyssar-Frank includes a chapter on Richardson entitled "Black Playwright for Two Worlds: Willis Richardson's *The Broken Banjo* and *The Chip Woman's Fortune*." To her, Richardson is important as "the first black writer to make a serious commitment to drama for and about black life." She connects his work to the "allegorical strain in contemporary Black Revolutionary Theatre and to the attention given the lives of the 'lowly' found in contemporary theater of 'black experience' "(21). Further, Keyssar-Frank acknowledges the "unabashed educative strategy" in Richardson's plays (21). In *The Development of Black Theater in America: From Shadows to Selves* (1988), Leslie Sanders includes a chapter on Richardson entitled "How Shall the Negro Be Portrayed?" In it, she states that Richardson's work "provided a base for subsequent black theater" (61).

That his plays are worthy of much closer scrutiny than they have received is acknowledged by Arthur P. Davis. An African-American scholar who wrote several books on African-American literature, Davis was coeditor of *The Negro Caravan* (1941), one of the first anthologies of African-American literature. In a letter to the author, Davis wrote, "I should have written about [Willis] Richardson as a pioneer African-American dramatist. . . . My neglect of [him] is a *sore spot* in my scholarly life." As will be discussed, Richardson's plots and conflicts mark his work as distinctly different from that of his contemporaries. In addition, his plays contain characters and situations that are prototypes, in several instances, of plays by Hansberry and subsequent black dramatists. Through the example of Richardson, this book, then, explores how African Americans related, on their own terms, their own version of life in the early years of twentieth-century America.

NOTES

1. I use the terms "black" and "African American" interchangeably. By black drama, I mean plays that were written by blacks, not plays about black culture that were written by whites. For consistency, I have chosen not to capitalize the words "black" and "white."

2. For an annotated bio-bliography of early African-American drama, see Bernard L. Peterson, Jr., *Early Black American Playwrights and Dramatic Writers: A Biographical Directory and Catalog of Plays, Films, and Broadcasting Scripts* (Westport, CT: Greenwood Press, 1990).

1

"All Within My Power": The Biography of Willis Richardson

❖

Remember that what you are told is really threefold: shaped by the teller, reshaped by the listener, and concealed from both by the dead man.

Vladimir Nabokov,
The Real Life of Sebastian Knight

Assembling an accurate biography of Willis Richardson is difficult. Gaps are left open, details go unsupported, and in some cases, Richardson seems to have been intentionally misleading. Various questions his family had, and still have, will, it seems, never be answered. He seems to have wanted it that way, for he avoided revealing his background. Rather than tell his life story as it actually was, he often shaped parts of it to align with what he wished it had been. In writing about him, I must, therefore, frequently rely on "seems" and "perhaps."

His evasion is evident in his opening to a letter, written in 1965, to Thomas Jervay, editor of *The Journal*, a black-owned newspaper in Richardson's hometown of Wilmington, North Carolina. Appearing hesitant to reveal too much about himself, Richardson opened a letter concerning details of his life with the noncommittal "As far as I know. . . . " The sketch of his life he later submitted to a

newspaper ends with his recollection of winning the Edith Schwab
Cup at Yale University in 1928, nearly four decades earlier, for his
play *The Chip Woman's Fortune*. In his 35-page unpublished autobiography, "From Youth to Age," Richardson skimmed over the last
thirty years of his life. Believed to have been written around 1970,
the manuscript contains only a one-page, spotty summary of his
life after 1935. It appears that he thought little of his life was worth
recording beyond his activities in the 1920s and 1930s, for those
years are highly detailed with the names of drama groups and the
titles, dates, and locations of productions.

His family questions aspects of his early life that he recorded in
his autobiography. Richardson wrote that he was born in Wilmington, North Carolina, on 5 November 1889. His family, however, believes that he may have been born on an island off the coast of South
Carolina, for he often spoke of growing up hearing the Geechie dialect, a black speech idiom native to that area.

The identity of his biological parents is also difficult to deter-
mine. His mother, at least in name, was Agnes Ann Harper Richardson. She worked at home and appears to have been devoted to
her son. His family, however, disputes her relationship to him,
holding that Agnes Harper was actually Richardson's grandmother and that Julia, who was said to be Richardson's much-older
sister, "was in fact his mother." Perhaps he was aware of this and
ashamed by it, for Julia is never mentioned in any of his papers.

Questions arise also about Richardson's father. Willis Wilder, his
father in name, was a laborer in a Wilmington brickyard. Wilder is
thought to have been well read and involved in black politics in
that city. Although Wilder raised Richardson as his son, the family
believes that the playwright's biological father was a wealthy
white man, a Mr. McKoy, of Wilmington. In going through the papers of Agnes Harper on her death, Jean Hall, Richardson's only
surviving daughter, noticed that Richardson's name was recorded
on the insurance certificate as Willis McKoy. The family story is that
McKoy promised Richardson's family that the boy could have
"anything he wanted monetarily, scholastically" for his upbringing
if the child carried the McKoy name. Whether out of shame or his
ignorance of this, Richardson never mentioned Mr. McKoy to anyone. In later comments, Richardson noted the influence Willis
Wilder had on his youth, writing that he was "one of the three most

important people in [his] life" and his "guide." Richardson's biography, however, seems to belie this, for beyond childhood, little mention is made of his father, including Willis Wilder's death. In fact, after the family's move to Washington, D.C., in 1899, Wilder is barely referred to in Richardson's autobiography.

Despite the enigma of his parentage, Richardson's childhood in Wilmington seems to have been the happiest, least-troubled period of his life. "I was born in good circumstances," he recalled in 1974. "I didn't ever experience any great poverty" (Willis).[1] Reared in a one-story house on Nixon Street, Richardson wrote, "We had a good house, good furniture, good food, and good clothes, and I had all the toys that a small boy could desire" ("Youth"). He attended Mrs. Moore's "pay [sic] school" at the age of five and recalls being read fairy tales by his father. The Richardson household appears to have been both secure and peaceful during his very early years.

An event in the fall of 1898, however, unsettled the family, as it must have all black families in that coastal area of North Carolina. In 1898, the Wilmington Riots broke out, resulting in the deaths of sixteen blacks. This event no doubt had an impact on the 10-year-old boy, for he records it in great detail in his autobiography and notes that "Thursday, November 10 [1898], is a day I shall never forget." In supporting editor Hoke Smith's campaign for governor of Georgia, part of which was to take the vote away from blacks, the *Atlanta Journal* published sensationalized stories of alleged crimes by blacks that included rape and "instances of arrogance" against whites (Woodward 86). These stories led to racial tension in Wilmington before the election that fall. Richardson recalled that two days prior to the election, "the white newspaper dared the Black men to come to the polls to vote" ("Youth"). The black men, he records, weren't "scared," because "at that time, it wasn't against the rules for a man to carry a gun in his pocket." On election day the African Americans voted. Shortly after the election, 400 Red Shirts, a faction of the Ku Klux Klan, invaded the black districts of Wilmington.

Willis Wilder is presumed to have been among the many blacks who were sought by the gang, for Richardson recounted that his father told a neighbor "he was sure the Red Shirts would come for him [Wilder] that night." Richardson later learned that his father "had been marked for death because he voted and encouraged other Black men to vote." Richardson wrote,

After the morning's carnage a dreadful silence hovered over the city. Those who had committed murder melted into the white community, hid their rifles and became respectable citizens. There was no investigation, no one was blamed, no one was punished. No white person [came forward] about the dreadful murderers. ("Youth")

At home during that bloody night, Willis Wilder sat at the kitchen table defending his household with a loaded revolver, a rifle, and several boxes of cartridges as he read *A Progress of a Race* (1892), a book that exhorted blacks to work as seamstresses and laborers to gain financial success.[2] Memories of the bloody episode in Wilmington and of his father literally guarding the hearth shaped some of the decisions Richardson later made for his plays.

Shortly after the riots, Wilder decided that the family should leave Wilmington. "Over Boston, Philadelphia, and Baltimore, he chose Washington, D.C., as the most favorable city" because several of Wilder's friends lived there. That spring, Wilder left the family in Wilmington and sought living quarters for them in the District of Columbia. Richardson and his mother left Wilmington in August for what, as Richardson writes, they "hoped would be the promised land." On arriving in Norfolk, they took an all-night steamboat up the Chesapeake Bay to the Potomac River and into the Capital. After moving his family there, it is believed that Wilder returned to Wilmington to complete the sale of the family's house.

Discrepancies arise in regard to Wilder and the home in Wilmington. His family recounts stories of a white man in Wilmington who had urged the family to move and who offered to sell the house for them. It is believed that this person sold the house and kept the money. Some family members disagree, saying that when Willis Wilder returned to Wilmington several years later, he was killed for his earlier involvement in the riots. Other family members believe that he may have deserted the family. In an interview given in 1977, however, Richardson gave a much less dramatic story, commenting that his father was "in charge of the engine room at Woodward and Lothrop," a department store in Washington, D.C. (Garvin). Aside from these details, no others are ever recorded about his father or their relationship. No family member recalls Willis Wilder, who may have died before 1925. His role in Richardson's life may never be clarified. The family believes that Agnes Harper Richardson, his mother in name, died of stomach cancer in the Richardson home in 1920. Little is known of her life or death.

One influence Wilder had was in encouraging Richardson's interest in books and writing by reading to the young boy. His family notes that although reading was important to Richardson in his youth, Julia and Agnes Harper Richardson were believed to have been illiterate. As a child, Richardson recalls that he was frequently criticized by neighbors for reading too much: "I used to forget the rest of the world and become a part of the adventures of Frank and Dick Merriwell, Old King Brady, the Liberty Boys of Seventy-six, the James Boys, and others too numerous to mention" ("Youth"). He writes that the "watchword" in his family had always been "learn." He was told that if he couldn't recite the alphabet backward he didn't know it and that if he couldn't read a book upside down he wasn't able to read. At times, riding the streetcar to school, he would read a book in such a manner, drawing puzzled stares from other passengers.

The family moved several times within Washington, D.C., so, as Richardson recorded, his father could "come into contact with men he could talk to [about] history, religion and politics." The Richardson family first lived in a second-floor apartment at Fourth and P streets in the District, and, after several other locations, finally settled at 410 I (Eye) Street.

The dates of Richardson's education are not clear. In September 1899, he completed the seventh grade at the Slater School.[3] He then went to the Jones School, which several of his friends attended. On 30 May 1906, he won for the school its first athletic medal in a city-wide competition. In his autobiography, Richardson wrote that he entered the M Street School in September 1906. However, in a 1975 letter to a newspaper editor, Richardson wrote that he "was enrolled in M Street High School in September 1899."

According to his family, the M Street School and W.E.B. Du Bois were among the most important influences on Richardson's life. Jean Hall points out that her father "had an unusual education for that time." Founded in 1870, the M Street School, later named Dunbar High School, was the first public high school for blacks in the

United States. With its high standards, the school was equal aca-
demically to the nation's exclusive preparatory schools attended
by children of wealthy white parents, and its students frequently
became doctors or lawyers and entered leadership positions. Students there studied English, Latin, French, German, history, and
music—atypical subjects for a race still fighting lynching and Jim
Crow beyond the school's boundaries. The high admission standards made admission possible for only the brightest, most promising students, all of whom were thoroughly interviewed as part of
the application process (Anderson 96).

During his senior year at the school, Richardson set records as
champion marksman for black schools in the Washington, D.C.,
area. At the M Street School, he was captain of both the football
team and the school's cadet company. Despite these laurels, Richardson must have been perceived by himself and others as an out-
sider. Not only a site of rigorous academic standards, the school
drew students from the black elite of Washington, D.C. Students
might have coming-out parties, shop in New York City, and spend
their summers in Europe. Clearly, Richardson, whose mother, it is
believed, was illiterate and whose father was a manual laborer at a
prestigious department store, did not have the means to maintain
even the pretense of fitting in.

At the school, however, Richardson had contact with people
who would become significant both in African-American literature
and culture and in his development as a dramatist.[4] Anna Julia
Cooper (1858–1964), an African-American feminist and scholar,
served as the school's principal from 1902 to 1906 and taught Latin
there from 1910 to 1924. Founder of Negro History Week in 1916,
Carter G. Woodson (1875–1950), taught history at the school from
1909 to 1918. Woodson would later hire Richardson as an editor of
two anthologies of black plays. Playwright Mary Burrill
(1884–1946) taught English and encouraged Richardson, one of her
prize students, in his writing. She would be instrumental in having
Richardson's first play read and evaluated by Alain Locke.[5] Angelina Grimké (1880–1958), an English teacher at the school, had an
informal relationship with Richardson and reviewed some of his
poems before he began writing plays. Her play *Rachel* would give
Richardson the initial impetus for his career as a dramatist. Edward
Christopher Williams, the school's principal from 1909 to 1916,

would critique one of Richardson's first plays and later collaborate with him on *The Chasm* (1926), a one-act play.[6]

After graduation from the M Street School, many students went on to Howard University, considered the premiere African-American university. In *Beyond Civil Rights*, a book on the work of Russell and Rowena Jelliffe, founders of the Karamu House in Cleveland, John Selby writes that Richardson taught English at Howard University (57). Richardson, however, never attended Howard University or any post-secondary school. Because his family needed the income the teenager could bring in, he had to turn down the scholarship offered to him by the university.[7] Although he did not attend Howard, Richardson must have told friends that he had. His family remarked that he was not invited to the reunion of students from the M Street School because he told the reunion committee that he had graduated from Howard University.

Instead of continuing with his education after high school, Richardson worked briefly as a "burnisher of pictures" for J.F. Jarvis in Washington, D.C. He maintained his contact with Williams, who soon recommended him for a job at the Library of Congress. Richardson worked there during December 1910 as an assistant to Lee Phillips, the chief of the Division of Maps and Charts. Because Richardson had studied French, his tasks included stack searches for French texts for Phillips. Although he was there only briefly, Richardson interest in writing was stirred; it was something he had been interested in but had considered "far beyond anything [he] could have imagined." Through his stint at the Library of Congress, Richardson was, as his wrote in his autobiography, in "contact with all those books [which] caused [him] to yearn for a writing career" ("Youth"). At Phillips's suggestion, Richardson taught himself to type, which he practiced by copying Tennyson's poems. At the encouragement of Phillips, Richardson wanted to "write something of [his] own" ("Youth").

In February 1911, he received a letter from the Bureau of Engraving and Printing in response to a job application he had submitted two years earlier. He was hired as a "skilled helper" in the wetting division of the Bureau in March 1911. Richardson recalled being told by a black administrator at the time that "not many men of our race [are] fortunate enough to get such a good start in life." Beginning in the 19th century, the Bureau was "one of the few places where Blacks were hired" ("Youth"). He had what his family referred to as a "subsidized job." According to his work records, he made only minimal advances within the division during his forty-four years there. During his first few years there, he earned $2.11 each day; his employment records show only slight increases annually in his hourly wage. In this low-level position, his main duty was to register the sheets of paper Bureau employees used for printing scrip. As Richardson recalled in an interview,

The people had to come to the door [each morning] for a certain number of sheets [of paper] . . . and I would then be free for a couple of hours. They wouldn't come up for paper to print for the afternoon until around three o'clock. I would write when I didn't have anything else to do. (Garvin)

Although his position was menial, it supported his family and gave him a modicum of status because it was a government job and it did not require outside manual labor. He remarked that it was the "best job in the building," because it allowed him time to write "more than the average playwright [does] in a lifetime" (Garvin). In 1912, Richardson met his future wife, Mary Ellen Jones, another Bureau employee.[8] They were married in the District of Columbia on 14 September 1914 when he was 26 years old. At that time, he converted to Roman Catholicism, which was his wife's religion.

He notes in his autobiography that he had heard that every writer began by writing poetry because it is "the first of the written arts" ("Youth"). He soon found out, however, that he "knew nothing about poetic technique." To remedy this, in 1915 Richardson enrolled in "Poetry and Versification," a two-year correspondence course from the Home Correspondence School in Springfield, Massachusetts.[9] Although interested in poetry, Richardson was to discover in 1916 that his strength lay in writing plays.

In March of that year, he and Oscar Bohannan, a young poet and close friend, attended Angelina Grimké's play *Rachel*.[10] Seeing the play was a turning point in Richardson's life, for the production led him to consider writing plays, a decision that would bring him both great joy and great disappointment. Walking home from that evening's production, Richardson commented to Bohannan that while *Rachel* was "a good play," he felt that together they "could do something better" (Garvin). When Bohannan moved to New York within the next few months to study music, Richardson enrolled at the same correspondence school in a course on writing plays.[11] His plans to collaborate with Bohannan never took shape. After reading a "thousand books on plays and playwrighting [sic]," he began writing his own material ("Youth").

By the fall of 1919, just over three years after seeing *Rachel*, Richardson must have contacted *Crisis* magazine, for that November the magazine published his essay "The Hope of a Negro Drama." In this, the first of his six essays on the theater, Richardson criticized plays written by blacks for white audiences, citing *Rachel* as an example of such a play. He wrote that it "shows the manner in which Negroes are treated by white people in the United States." Richardson believed, instead, that plays written by African Americans should focus on the black community and not on racial tensions and differences. In the essay, he mentioned the course that most of his plays would take: drawn for the most part from the folk tradition, they would center on conflicts within the black community.

By 1921, three daughters had been born to the Richardsons, and the family had moved to 2023 Thirteenth Street in Washington, D.C., where he would live until his death in 1977.[12] He recorded that through his kitchen door, he could see the backstage entrance of the Lincoln Theater, a theater popular for its musicals ("Youth"). Perhaps this doorway reminded him of the stereotypes of blacks popularized in song and dance productions that held back the race.

In his autobiography, Richardson wrote that he considered "Dr. Du Bois the greatest and most brilliant black man this country has yet produced," calling him "my philosopher" ("Youth"). As Richardson's family recollects, only two photographs ever hung on his bedroom wall: one of a Watusi woman in full native dress and the other of Du Bois. Although they are believed to have had contact only briefly, Du Bois was a crucial influence in Richardson's life. As editor of *Crisis*, Du Bois had published Richardson's first essay, "The Hope of a Negro Drama" (1919). In December 1920, Du Bois published Richardson's first play for children, *The King's Dilemma*, in *The Brownies' Book*, a magazine that Du Bois had helped found. Du Bois, Richardson recalled, "wanted these plays for that *Brownies' Book*, 1922, I think. He wrote to me and asked if I could write them" (Garvin). Over the next year Richardson wrote four one-act children's plays for the publication: *The King's Dilemma* (December

1920), *The Gypsy's Finger-Ring* (March 1921), *The Children's Treasure* (June 1921), and *The Dragon's Tooth* (Oct. 1921). These would later be included in his collection of plays for children, *The King's Dilemma: Episodes of Hope and Dream*, which was published in 1956. The Deacon's Awakening, his first play for an older audience was published in *Crisis* in November 1920 and was first produced on 1 January 1921 at a union hall in St. Paul, Minnesota.

In addition to Du Bois, E. C. Williams was among those who first recognized Richardson's ability. Williams had been involved in Richardson's life at several points: as his high school Latin teacher and as his former principal at the M Street School. In 1916, Williams became a librarian at Howard University, where he worked until his death in 1929. Richardson writes, "I knew Mr. Williams was well-versed in playwrighting [*sic*] because I had seen one of his plays [*Lorenzo the Magnificent*] staged at the Howard Theater" ("Youth" 31). After reading Richardson's play *The Idle Head*, Williams declared it "the best play he had seen written by a member of our race" and asked to see other plays Richardson had written. He suggested that Richardson show manuscripts of *The Idle Head* and *The Broken Banjo* to Mary Burrill, Richardson's former English teacher.[13] Seeing his promise as a black playwright, Burrill asked whether she, along with Alain Locke and Montgomery Gregory, who had organized the Howard University Players, might hear a reading of the plays. As Richardson wrote, "We went to her [Burrill's] apartment one night, and they were enthused about the plays. They thought they had found a playwright" ("Youth").

It is important to keep in mind the distinction between the Howard Theater, which was founded on 22 August 1910, and the Howard University Players. Although, the Howard Theater was located near the university, the theater was neither part of nor associated with the Howard University Theater. The school's theater group, officially formed in 1922, was part of the school's English Department. It had never produced a play written by an African American other than those by Gregory's students. The possibility of engaging an African-American playwright, one who wrote plays on black life, stimulated the Department of Dramatic Arts, which had only recently been established at the school.

All signs in 1921 pointed toward a promising future for the fledgling theater group at Howard University. Headed by Marie

Moore-Forrest, who was assisted by Cleon Throckmorton, the new drama group, it was hoped, would "enable the Negro to express in artistic form the finer aspects of his racial life." Among the purposes of the department was producing plays "largely written by Negroes and acted by them" ("Notes"). These plays, it was believed, would "enable the race to win respect" (Moore-Forrest 1). Despite the hopes for and promise of the African-American stage, the problem remained that African-American playwrights were scarce. Understandably then, Locke and Gregory were enthusiastic about Richardson's submission. Eugene O'Neill's "Negro plays," as well as those by the white playwright Ridgely Torrence, had piqued the interest of white playwrights in writing about and exploring African-American culture for source materials. Gregory frequently invited Richardson to rehearsals of the plays in production at the university. In December 1922, Gregory wrote to Richardson: "The sun is just beginning to shine on Negro art and I am encouraged to believe that this year will see even finer things." The excitement, however, was soon dampened, as Richardson's submissions were turned down for production. As he explained,

Locke and Gregory had a difficult time getting the consent of the [white] president of the university [Stanley Durkee] and the head of the English department. It was quite all right for them to stage a play written by a white writer at a Black university, but a play by a Black writer [who was not a student] was too rare to be considered. (32)

It would take an outside success for Richardson's work before a play of his would appear on stage at Howard University. Du Bois made this success possible for Richardson by arranging for one of his plays to be produced by the Ethiopian Art Theater, a theater group in Chicago that had written to Du Bois, asking if he knew of any plays written by blacks. Richardson recalled that Raymond O'Neil, who had organized the Ethiopian Art Players, "was looking for one-act plays by Negroes, and he contacted Dr. Du Bois . . . [who] asked me to write to [Raymond] O'Neil, and I sent him *The Chip Woman's Fortune* and *The Broken Banjo*" (Garvin). Published in *Crisis* in 1922, *The Chip Woman's Fortune* opened in Chicago on 23 January 1923. The play began a two-week run at the Howard Theater on 30 April 1923, the crowd growing larger each evening. Unable to locate a theater for the play in central New York City, O'Neil, the drama group's manager, had the play produced on 7 May 1923 at Harlem's Lafayette Theater, the first New York City theater to desegregate. Still without a theater near Broadway, the group returned to the Howard Theater for another week. On 15 May 1923, the Frazee Theater in New York presented as a triple bill Shakespeare's *The Comedy of Errors*, Oscar Wilde's *Salomé*, and *The Chip Woman's Fortune*. The date is significant in African-American theater history as the first time a play by an African American had been produced on Broadway.

After a two-week run, however, O'Neil absconded with the proceeds, and the series closed. The theater, Richardson recalled, "almost had a riot," when the audience, reacting to the unannounced change, demanded their money back. Raymond O'Neil "had left town with the money, leaving the players stranded in New York." Richardson noted that O'Neil's theft "ruined the Ethiopian Art Players; they broke up after that" (Garvin). Despite this misfortune, Richardson's play ran long enough to garner favorable reviews, which meant that Richardson would meet with less resistance in realizing one of his dreams, having his work produced at Howard University:

[After] the rave notices about my play in New York, Washington and Chicago, Locke and Gregory decided that the powers at Howard University could no longer deny a play of mine a showing on the stage of the university. So in 1924 *Mortgaged* . . . was staged for the entertainment of the students and the community. ("Youth")

Aside from student productions, *Mortgaged* was the first play written by an African American to be staged at Howard University. Over the next several years, *The House of Sham*, *Compromise*, *The Chip Woman's Fortune*, and other plays by Richardson were produced there.

In 1925, Richardson was informed that he had placed first in the Krigwa Literary Contest, sponsored by *Crisis*, for *The Broken Banjo*. Eugene O'Neill, one of the judges for the awards, remarked that he was "glad the judges all agree on *The Broken Banjo*. . . . Willis Richardson should certainly continue working in his field."[14] Unable to attend the ceremonies in New York for the play, Richardson was awarded the same prize the following year for his play *The Boot-black Lover*. It was at that ceremony that the playwright met Du Bois, his spiritual mentor. While in New York, Richardson stayed with his friend Bohannan, who was living in Harlem with his (Bohannan's) high school English teacher, much to Richardson's disbelief.[15]

After the appearance of several plays and essays in *Crisis*, *Opportunity*, and *The Messenger*, publications directed to black readers, good fortune continued for Richardson. Little-theater groups and schools throughout the country sought his one-act plays for their benefits, class activities, English departments, and church drama groups. During the 1920s, through his contacts at Howard University, Richardson began joining other artists and writers at the Saturday Nighters, an informal group that met at the home of Washington poet and playwright Georgia Douglas Johnson.[16] Richardson was involved with the group from its formation in 1926 until it disbanded ten years later. Du Bois, Langston Hughes, Jean Toomer, Mary Church Terrell, Carter Woodson, James Weldon Johnson, Zora Neale Hurston, and the illustrator of *The New Negro*, Aaron Douglas, were among the many poets and writers who gathered at Johnson's home. According to Richardson,

Every Saturday night a group of us would go over there and talk over things we had done or planned to do. We used to meet at nine o'clock and stay until two or three in the morning and discuss things, like writing; some would read their poems and they would discuss them. . . . Whenever Du Bois or Hughes was in town, they would come. (Garvin)

Weekly, several playwrights gathered with Richardson at Johnson's home—Marita Bonner, Eulalie Spence, Georgia Johnson, May Miller, who later played in *The Broken Banjo*, Randolph Edmonds, Carrie Clifford, and E. C. Williams. These playwrights were all involved to some extent with the Krigwa Players, a little-theater organization created and encouraged by Du Bois.

Committed to the value of the stage in uniting and in teaching African Americans, Du Bois saw the Krigwa groups as a means of bringing together African Americans through their involvement in the community-based Krigwa little-theater groups. Richardson recalled,

Dr. Du Bois rode around to different places promoting the idea of Black theater. . . . *Crisis* was the main way for plays to become known. Du Bois organized the Krigwa Players, which were quite successful. We began in 1927 and went until 1935, [with one branch] on the West coast and [others] in Cleveland and Chicago and lots of large cities. (Undated notes)

Jean Richardson Hall, Richardson's youngest daughter, writes that until 1935 "Dad had a group called the Krigwaw [sic] Players who rehearsed at our house. They did Dad's plays and the plays of other playwrites [sic]." Richardson's wife, nicknamed Morse (which was pronounced Moss), served as Krigwa's secretary until the group disbanded in 1935.

In 1926, the Gilpin Players, a black little-theater group at Karamu House in Cleveland, produced Richardson's play *Compromise*, the group's first production by an African-American playwright.[17] Rowena Jelliffe, the group's founder, remarked in an interview shortly before her death in 1992 that "Richardson's play was the first bright spot on the Karamu stage."[18]

Although no other play by Richardson ever appeared on Broadway, other successes came his way. Through his involvement with the Drama Department at Howard University and the appearance of his plays in *Crisis*, Richardson began building a reputation as a playwright, and the demand for his plays increased. Schools, church groups, and neighborhood associations produced *Compromise, Mortgaged*, and *The Broken Banjo*, and Locke included *Flight of the Natives* in his anthology *Plays of Negro Life* (1927).

In 1924, Richardson's fortune began to change. Gregory left Howard University to accept the position of Superintendent of Schools for Newark, New Jersey. As the director of the Howard Players, Gregory had been an important force in the school's theater program and a vital connection for Richardson in having his plays produced there. His relationship with Gregory was not nearly as important to Richardson's future, however, as his relationship with Locke had been. In an interview, the playwright recalled that he used to visit Locke's home frequently. He noted that Locke "kept the most ragged apartment with books on the floor and chairs, so many [books] he couldn't handle them all" (Willis). His admiration for Locke was based not only on the help Locke, via the Howard Theater Department, had given him. Richardson also respected Locke for what had been accomplished with his 1925 publication: "That book [*The New Negro*] introduced new Negroes, or new Black writers, to the public . . . the white people didn't notice anybody but Paul Lawrence [*sic*] Dunbar [before that]" (Unpublished notes).

Although Richardson acknowledged that Locke was a "brilliant man" and that Locke had helped him immeasurably in his early productions, Richardson recounted a falling out that severed their relationship, a break that, however petty in retrospect, damaged Richardson's efforts to have his plays, if not produced, then published. Locke apparently produced *Compromise* without seeking Richardson's permission. After learning of the production, Richardson contacted Locke: "Since the school didn't [give credit to] me at all, I wrote a letter [to Locke] asking for five dollars for staging that play. Locke was the man who gave them permission to stage it. [We had] no contact after that" (Garvin).

This broken tie seems to have damaged Richardson, for few of his plays received the same attention and publicity they had through the Howard Players. Also, Locke's nurturing of black writers was widely known and his influence widespread; to be shunned by him no doubt lessened many opportunities Richardson may have otherwise had. Shortly after the incident, Sterling Brown, who taught English at Howard, had his assistant contact Richardson about contributing a play to the anthology *The Negro Caravan* (1941). Edited by Arthur P. Davis and Brown, the anthology was intended for African-American students who were unable to find literature written by African Americans. Locke must have contacted either Brown or Davis at some point, for the play was returned to Richardson without comment. As Richardson noted, "By that time Locke had stopped speaking to me" (Garvin). The break with Locke seems also to have wounded Richardson both emotionally and creatively, for after that point he recorded little of his life in detail. Existing records and evidence of his commitment to drama are largely the notes he scrawled on legal pads and on the backs of envelopes. He meticulously recorded numerous sites and dates of productions play by play, as though he were wringing what memories he could from his days of relative success. After being shunned by Locke, Richardson's productivity seemed to fall off, as further productions were mostly of plays he had written years earlier.

His relationship with Carter G. Woodson, however, proved to be of immense value. By 1929, Richardson had agreed to work for Woodson, known as the "Father of Negro History," in collecting and editing a group of plays. Published in 1930, *Plays and Pageants from the Life of the Negro* was the first anthology of plays by African Americans. His introduction and four of his plays appeared in this volume. In response to the number of requests for and the lack of teaching materials on African-American history, Woodson had Richardson collect several plays on black history. These were to be produced by school and church theater groups. Published in 1935, *Negro History in Thirteen Plays* included five plays by Richardson. Both collections were published by Associated Publishers, an African-American publishing firm in Washington, D.C., for which Woodson was editor.

Richardson's plays were staged throughout the United States during the 1930s and occasionally queries from people outside the United States arrived at his home on Thirteenth Street. In 1931, a newspaper in Budapest wrote for permission to publish *Compromise*:

I follow with great interest the negro litereture [*sic*]; some years ago [I] have also written to Mr. Du Bois for informations [*sic*] in this line. . . . The publication of your play could contribute to earnest knowledge of true negro art and mentality in our country, both of which I am eager to propagate. (Kobor)

A Brother Bernardine in "Entebbe, Uganda," wrote to him in 1938, requesting a copy, "even second-hand," of *Negro History in Thirteen Plays*. And Richardson's plays were still produced well into the 1930s at black colleges and by black little-theater groups throughout the southeastern United States. He continued writing plays and began a series of autobiographical short stories, the Banny Simms stories.

Despite the notice his plays received through Woodson's publications, Richardson's work seems to have been dismissed by those who might have helped him. Lester Walton had at one time, possibly during the 1930s, shown interest in producing Richardson's plays for the Lafayette Players, the first black stock theater group in Harlem. Richardson recalled, "Right before President Roosevelt appointed [Walton] as ambassador to Liberia for eight years or more, he had written to me and tried to get things going; he could have done a lot for me" (Willis). On leaving for his assignment, Walton had Richardson send his plays to George Norford, a playwright who had helped found the Rose McClendon Players in 1938. "I sent him a group of one-act plays," Richardson recalled. "He kept them for 14 months and then sent them back with no explanation" (Garvin). It must have been with some bitterness that Richardson read Montgomery Gregory's 1940 letter to him: "You pioneered Negro theater, but unfortunately very few have followed your splendid example." Eighteen years earlier, Richardson had written to Gregory that he would "do all within [his] power to advance Negro drama." Few of his efforts, it seems, had paid off.

Aside from two events, the 1940s were generally a calm period in Richardson's life.[19] His respect for and, although distant, his relationship with Du Bois put Richardson, according to his family, "left of center" politically. A member of the National Association for the Advancement of Colored People, the Urban League, and the United Federation of Labor, Richardson and his real or suspected leftist sympathies apparently raised the suspicions of his employer, the federal government. His family remarked that Richardson was a socialist, but not active in the party. They believe that in the early 1920s, during the Palmer raids, his desk was searched and his correspondence with Du Bois was "looked at."[20] Although his work records do not mention this, they do contain several affidavits Richardson signed pledging loyalty to the U.S. government and that he was not engaged in any strike against the government. On 11 September 1947, he signed a loyalty oath for the Bureau.[21] The more important event of the decade was also one of Richardson's greatest personal tragedies. On 7 March 1947, Noel, his youngest daughter, committed suicide. The tragedy was compounded by the refusal of Saint Augustine's Church to bury her. The Richardsons' parish church, Saint Augustine's was affiliated with the Oblate Sisters of Providence, an order of African-American nuns located outside Baltimore. Richardson's daughter Shirley interceded, and Noel was buried by another Catholic church. Noel and her children, Joyce and Noel Lois, had lived with the Richardsons; upon Noel's death, they raised the children, officially adopting them in 1952.

In the early 1950s, sick and aging relatives moved into the Richardson home. Richardson was concerned with other things than the letter Rowena Jelliffe had written to him in December 1951, in which she thanked him for the copies of his plays and manuscripts he had donated to Karamu House.[22] On retiring from the Bureau on 31 March 1954, Richardson again attempted to get his work before the public. He compiled and republished the children's plays he had written over thirty years earlier for *The Brownies' Book* and added new plays. Published in 1955 by Associated Publishers in Washington, D.C., the collection was titled *The King's Dilemma*. In addition, he revised five of his earlier one-act plays, expanding them to three acts. Toward the end of the 1950s, it is believed that black filmmaker and lyricist Leigh Whipper, then in his 80s, asked Richardson if he could act as Richardson's agent in getting his plays produced.[23] Whipper had written several musicals and had been involved in the theater since 1899; he knew enough people in theater to revive Richardson's dream of having his plays produced. According to Richardson's notes, Whipper collected $10,000 to stage *The Amateur Prostitute* with the prospect that it would go to Broadway. Hopes dissolved, however, when Whipper reported to Richardson that more money was needed; the financial backing was never found.

Issues related to African Americans continued to provoke responses from the playwright. Richardson would not allow Coca Cola in his home because, as his family recalls, "the plant in Atlanta wouldn't hire Blacks." Humiliated and wounded by racism, Richardson distributed information from the NAACP and the Urban League to his granddaughters. He refused to see the movie *The Learning Tree* because its racist tones were "painful history for him" (Joyce Richardson letter, 10 October 1993). His attempts to educate his family about Paul Laurence Dunbar and Phillis Wheatley frustrated him because of the lack of available information on them.

With the arrival of the late 1960s, Richardson, never outwardly militant, was puzzled by the Black Power Movement: It was not the way he thought "it should be." More than the changes and events of the 1960s, the most difficult situation he faced professionally concerned the theater. Audiences had different tastes and interests. *A Raisin in the Sun* (1959) he could understand; plays like Amiri Baraka's *The Slave* (1964) no doubt puzzled him. One can only wonder what Richardson might have thought of such plays as Ed Bullins's *Clara's Old Man* (1965) or Baraka's *J-E-L-L-O* (1970). It must have been evident to him that his plays had become period pieces. Through uncomplicated plots, Richardson had told a version of African-American life different from that presented in African-American drama during the 1960s and 1970s. There was little place and no demand for his work.

Still, Richardson tried several venues to get his work before the public, even sending copies to the New York Shakespeare Festival: "I sent six plays to Joe Papp's office; the reader said the plays had high quality but were more suitable for movies or television because of the change in scenery," he wrote to his granddaughter. At an editor's request, he rewrote *The Amateur Prostitute*, adding a scene, but the play was returned unread "because the first reader [who had liked it] was no longer employed there" (Garvin). After three rejection letters from Papp's office with returned manuscripts, Richardson, in poor health and approaching 80, wrote to his granddaughter Joyce: "When you come home [to Washington] I want you to take some scripts back to New York with you, so that you and your friends can read them. Perhaps one of your friends knows an agent who would be interested. Please excuse the [hand] writing."[24]

In November 1972, Richardson wrote to James V. Hatch at the Hatch-Billops Collection in New York City, asking whether Hatch knew anyone who might be interested in his work: "I have five three-act plays suitable for production. I know that it is immodest for me to state, but these are the best plays yet written by any member of my race." Richardson also contacted other theater companies and drama publishers.[25] Nothing developed. When the three-act version of *The Broken Banjo* was rejected, Richardson noted, "I haven't been able to get an agent." He revised the play again but to no avail. In November of that year, the Afro-American Studio in New York City produced *The Chip Woman's Fortune*. This single stroke of recognition, however, did little to ease the bitterness and rejection felt by the 83–year-old playwright.

Richardson became embittered by the lack of recognition his work received and by the lack of any sort of remuneration for his work. Toward the end of his life he consoled himself by pointing out that he would "rather have a play published than staged, because then it lasts a lifetime" (Willis). Although his plays had been included in several anthologies, when the plays were produced at black colleges and universities, his permission was never sought: "They would take the book and stage the play, but they won't pay anything for it. I know [my plays] have been staged hundreds of times" (Garvin). An English teacher from Jackson State University in Mississippi, he recorded, told him that *The Chip Woman's Fortune* had recently been produced there, yet neither payment nor acknowledgment followed. In a strange twist, Roosevelt High School, located outside Washington, D.C., and attended by Richardson's grandson, produced *The Broken Banjo*, a play for which Richardson had been awarded first place in for the 1925 *Crisis* Drama Awards. Because the teacher doubted that the child's grandfather had written the play, Richardson gave the boy a pen with the playwright's name on it to show to her.

Broken by a life of large disappointments and little recognition, Richardson found that his health, too, was failing. His wife was going blind, and her younger sister moved in to care for them. He had been falling frequently and was at times unable to stand. Diagnosed as having Padgett's disease (*osteitis deformans*), a progressive deterioration of bone, Richardson convalesced for several months during 1974 in a nursing home in Silver Spring, Maryland. The doctor told Richardson he was "the only lucid person there" and sent him home to Thirteenth Street. Because Richardson's library, which filled more than two rooms, had been a source of conflict between him and his wife, he had agreed to dispose of part of it. He returned from the convalescent home, however, to discover that his wife had instead donated it to a priest.[26] Aside from his plays, his books were his most prized possessions. Ironically, his library, or part of it, was at one time located at the convent of the Oblate Sisters of Providence outside Baltimore, the same order that had refused his daughter Noel a Catholic burial.[27] Left with only ten books, he commented to his granddaughter, "I might as well have committed suicide as to come home to this." Despairing, certain that all he had done and hoped for had been in vain, shortly before his death Richardson told an interviewer, "I figured I had written enough; if [theaters] couldn't stage any of [my plays], there wasn't anything I could do about it" (Garvin).

A lonely man throughout his life, Richardson grew closer to his family only after the onset of his illness as he became dependent physically. Shortly after his return from the convalescent home, he sold his 1937 Buick. He soon purchased a burial plot with four grave sites in Lincoln Cemetery. He died on 7 November 1977, an atheist.[28] He is buried between his daughter Noel and his wife. Ironically, on 21 November, two weeks after his death, Richardson and his work received some of the acclaim he had pursued during the latter half of his life: He was recognized as "Outstanding Pioneer" in black theater by AUDELCO, the Audience Development Committee, an organization in New York City promoting black theater.[29] There is some consolation in knowing that Richardson had learned of this award, but he must have seen it as too little that came, painfully, too, too late.

To Joyce Richardson, there were two Willis Richardsons: One was a self-centered, private person, a man who seemed interested only in writing plays. As an adult, she became acquainted, however, with the other man, the one who had been both deeply wounded by the circumstances of his life and misunderstood. Although his public self may have been admired, few people knew the internal universe of Willis Richardson. His granddaughter notes, "Here's this enormously energetic, creative person who [had] to get a job . . . in the Bureau of Engraving and Printing, and he [had] this whole other life [writing plays]" (Interview 14 February 1992).

His commitment unnoticed by nearly everyone, Richardson feared that he had broken his vow to "do all within [his] power" for black drama. In his mind, he had been either unappreciated or forgotten by those who had meant most to him and by those who had been the greatest influences in his life: his wife and children, his father and mother, Locke, Du Bois, and those in theater and publishing who could have produced his plays. "He spent all his time in his room at his typewriter," Joyce Richardson recalled. "He didn't have much to do with us; in so many ways he was remote," she commented, stating that she has "been resistant [to reading his work] because Pop loved the plays more than he loved his family" (Interview, 17 March 1992).

Richardson's background did not include the options that a life with money offers. Because of financial, social, or emotional difficulties, he was unable to grasp opportunities and take advantage of occasions that would have brought his dreams for his plays, and African-American drama in general, closer to reality. Internal and external struggles led Richardson to create a world of appearances, a world that made his life seem to be other than it actually was. He never seemed to recover from always being at the margins—of not attending college, of not receiving the recognition he was sure would be his, of remaining in a relatively low-status position during his 44 years at the Bureau, and of not having submissions of his later work accepted.

Aware of the noncommittal nature of his recollections, his family remarks that "he [hid] things that were embarrassing or shameful or unsavory or didn't fit what he wanted [them] to be; he made things up [about himself]." As family members point out, Richardson "created himself as he wished to be known." Joyce Richardson, a granddaughter and Noel's daughter, notes that the playwright "lived under many burdens: for instance, was he legitimate or not? Did he know his father or not?" Although "he was creative, I never believed what he told me," she noted. Before his death in 1977, Richardson confided to her that his "whole life [was] built on a fiction." In retrospect, she agreed, later labeling the unknown pieces of his life "part of the mystery of him."

Despite the fictions he created to maintain his dignity, Richardson managed his life and his family responsibly. He had converted to Catholicism when he and Mary Ellen Jones married, because "his wife came from a long line of super Catholics" (Hall interview). During the 1950s he was corresponding secretary of the Derby Club, a social organization in Washington, D.C., for African-American men.[30] In both 1933 and 1950, he was listed in *Who's Who in Colored America*. To support his family, he remained at the Bureau of Engraving and Printing for 44 years. Although his public self may have been admired, few people knew the man, for he allowed limited entrance to his private world.

With so many gaps and incongruities and with few remaining sources to verify the stories, Richardson's life is an enigma. Much of that, however, seems to be the way that he wanted it. His family recalls him as a private, closed person who spent much of his free time in his room typing, reading, and pacing the floor. From recollections of acquaintances, he was shy and self-effacing. From letters he wrote and interviews he gave in the 1970s, he seems to have been a gentle person, deferential and yet proud. Naomi Rice, a friend of Richardson's daughter Shirley, recalls that he was "a quiet man, reserved, a recluse, one who showed little emotion and gave only brief responses."

From that March evening in 1916, when he and Otto Bohannan discussed *Rachel* as they walked home from the play, until the 1970s, Richardson worked toward the development of African-American drama. The pride he had derived from the glow and success of the 1920s never, however, returned. During the last decade of his life, much of what he was involved in concerned propping up the image that had come from his success during that decade. Today one venue we have into Richardson's life and mind is through his plays. In his plots, conflicts, and characters, it seems, he opened his heart by writing about personal incidents and concerns that troubled him. Perhaps it is in his plays, then, that we will find and meet Willis Richardson.

NOTES

1. Passages marked "Willis" are from the interview of Willis Richard son conducted by Cassandra Willis on 5 March 1972. The taped interview is located at the Hatch-Billops Collection in New York City.

2. J. L. Nichols and William Crogman, the authors, advocated Booker T. Washington's philosophy of accommodation. That is, by starting at the bottom rung and laboring as, for example, laundresses and carpenters, African Americans could "prove" themselves and thereby earn the trust and respect of whites. Published initially in 1892, *Progress of the Race* was revised several times. Opening with a history of Africa, the book focuses on the growth and advancement of the African race in the United States in regard to education, business, and religion.

3. According to the *Encyclopedia of African American Civil Rights: From Emancipation to the Present*. (Ed. Charles D. Lowery and John F. Marszalek. Westport, CT: Greenwood Press, 1992), the Slater Fund was "established in 1882 with a million-dollar endowment by Connecticut industrialist John Fox Slater" (479–80). The fund's purpose was to elevate black Southerners through education. Richardson's grade school was named after the philanthropist.

4. Because "academic posts were closed even to those Blacks who had completed graduate work," the M Street School "appeared as a kind of salvation, and the best Black teachers from all over the country competed for posts" there (Birmingham 143).

5. Mary Burrill also encouraged another student, May Miller, to write plays. Miller would later share in the credit with Richardson for editing *Negro History in Thirteen Plays* (1935).

6. Richardson later remembered E.C. Williams as "a brilliant man but [one who] never got much credit for it. . . . He and [May] Miller's father [Kelly Miller] used to do research for Dr. Du Bois for his books." Williams, he wrote, "could teach seven languages and could speak five" ("Youth"). The head librarian at Howard University, Williams helped Du Bois classify documents Du Bois had collected in Europe for his planned book on the Negro soldier in World War I. Williams was a teacher and librarian at Howard from 1916 to 1929, when he unexpectedly died.

7. His family recalled that Williams, the principal at the M Street School, wrote to Richardson about this disappointment and added, "No, I can't give the scholarship to your friend."

8. Mary Ellen Jones was of Indian, white, and black ancestry. Her father, William Jones, a white man, had been born in Scotland; her mother, Sarah, was of white, Native American, and African descent.

9. His still-unpublished manuscript of sixty-four poems, entitled "Victorian Poems," is located in Harlem at the Schomburg Center for Research in Black Culture.

10. Grimké was the only child of Archibald Grimké (1849–1930). A former slave who became a distinguished journalist and diplomat, Grimké served as head of the Washington branch of the NAACP (Kellner 144).

11. Bohannan and Richardson's plans to write plays together never materialized. Richardson mentions him only once in his papers, recalling that he stayed with the poet when he went to New York in 1926 to accept the *Crisis* Drama Award.

12. His daughters are Jean Paula, born 7 August 1916; Shirley Antonella, born 29 April 1918; and Noel Justine, born 14 August 1920.

13. Burrill, too, had written plays, both of which addressed issues that directly affected the lives of African Americans in the early twentieth century. *They That Sit in Darkness*, published in the *Birth Control Review* in 1919, illustrated the need for birth-control information to be distributed among indigent women. In that same year, *The Liberator* published her play *Aftermath* about the discrimination blacks faced on returning from the war in Europe.

14. Quoted from "Willis Richardson." In Leo Hamalian and James V. Hatch, eds. *The Roots of African-American Drama: An Anthology of Early Plays, 1858–1938.* Detroit: Wayne State UP, 1991: 160. Among O'Neill's plays based on black life are *The Dreamy Kid*, *The Emperor Jones*, and *All God's Chillun Got Wings*.

15. In an interview, Richardson recalled winning his second and final prize in the *Crisis* literary contests: "In 1926 I sent another play of mine, *The Bootblack Lover*, to the contest, and in October Dr. Du Bois called and informed me that I had won first prize again, and invited me to come to the ceremonies" ("The Play Prizes").

16. Richardson noted in an interview that Georgia Johnson "was a poet [until] she found out people paid more attention to plays than poems" (Garvin interview).

17. Locke had helped Richardson with one of his plays, as a 1925 letter shows: "I thank you for the ending you have added to *Compromise*. I am sure whatever was done is an improvement to the play and your advice is always welcome" (Letter to Locke).

18. The Gilpin Players was an offshoot of Cleveland's Karamu Playhouse, which had been founded in 1915 in order to increase racial pride and awareness among African Americans. The Gilpin Players began with plays by whites and then, as cofounder Rowena Jelliffe noted, "the Negro had his own contribution to make to drama" (qtd. In Selby 192). The group sought to "develop the Negro's particular dramatic quality, to keep [the group] from being too contaminated by the western theatrical manner" (192). It focused on the development of African-American drama to this end. Karamu, a Swahili word meaning "place of joyful meeting," was organized in 1915 by Russell and Rowena Jelliffe, both white. This couple saw their mission as showing African Americans "what they have, what their ancestors had, what their heritage is. . . . [To show that African-American] roots are there to be proud of" (qtd. in Selby 5). As African Americans sought to improve the standards of their education, the Jelliffes used the stage as a way of reaching African-American students to teach them African and African-American history.

19. On 5 May 1941, his comic skit *Miss or Mrs.* was produced by the Bureau of Engraving Dramatic Club. In 1942, Richardson was listed in *Who's Who in the East*.

20. The Palmer "raids," as they were called, were conducted by Alexander Mitchell Palmer in the early 1930s. The U.S. Attorney General from 1919 to 1920, Palmer was known for zealously prosecuting those suspected of disloyalty to the United States.

21. In 1947, Richardson was admitted to the Authors' League of America and was, by this time, a member of the NAACP, the AFL, and the Urban League.

22. These items were given to the Hatch-Billops Archives in New York City in 1992, shortly after Rowena Jelliffe's death at the age of 100 that same year.

23. The source for this is a taped interview Richardson gave in 1975. No other mention is made of it in his letter, notes, or papers.

24. On 9 March, 15 May, 22 June 1973, Richardson received, respectively, rejection letters from the New York Shakespeare Festival for *The Amateur Prostitute*, *The Broken Banjo*, *The Visiting Lady*, and *Joy Rider*. On 5 February 1972, he received a rejection letter from Drama Book Specialists for *The Amateur Prostitute*. In March 1973, he joined the Harlem Arts Council.

25. His three-act plays are *The Broken Banjo*, *The Flight of the Natives*, *The Visiting Lady*, *Joy Rider*, and *The Amateur Prostitute*.

26. Naomi Rice, a friend of the Richardson family, remembered Richardson's library as being one of the largest she had ever seen as a child. In noting its size, she pointed out that "his extensive library covered the greater part of two rooms."

27. Through his wife, the family had several connections to this order. She was related to several of the nuns and had attended St. Cyprian's, the order's school in Washington, D.C. Noel Lois, Noel's daughter, had been a member of the order for five years.

28. Richardson may have become disillusioned with religion when the church refused to bury his daughter Noel, who had committed suicide.

29. According to playwright Woodie King, Richardson knew that he was going to receive this award. King also notes that Joyce Richardson gave a very moving speech on behalf of her grandfather (National Conference on African-American Theatre).

30. According to Thelma Hymen, a friend of the Richardson family, the Derby Club, located in Washington, D.C., is one of the oldest clubs for African-American men in that city. The social organization flourished from its founding in 1928 through the 1960s. Member Earnest Halton believes that Richardson was corresponding secretary during the 1960s. The club, he notes, was fairly formal, faithfully following Robert's Rules of Order. It was founded by well-to-do men of Washington, the black elite, and made up mostly of doctors and lawyers. The other social club in Washington was the Bachelor Benedicts. Although membership has fallen, both groups are still in existence.

2

The Mirror and the Mask: An Overview of African-American Drama during the 1920s

Before [the character of Invisible Man] could have some voice in his own destiny he had to discard these old identities and illusions. . . . The nature of our society is such that we are prevented from knowing who we are.

Ralph Ellison, "The Art of Fiction" 177

The three figures crucial both to Richardson's advancement as a dramatist and to the development of African-American drama are Alain Locke, W.E.B. Du Bois, and Carter G. Woodson. Although the three men disagreed on various topics in relation to black drama, they agreed that it needed to be developed and promoted. To them, the folk culture of black Americans was the source and the location of the black voice for the stage; for it was drawn from experiences familiar to blacks and from a culture beyond the ken of white playwrights. To Locke, plays based on African-American folk culture were a means of preserving, among other things, "the native optimism" and "joy of living" that he believed black folk culture had. To Du Bois, black folk plays were a means of reaching and thereby teaching an audience, and he believed that the stage should be used for educational purposes. Woodson heartily promoted the use of the black stage as a means of teaching African Americans about black history.

Despite the many pronouncements and promotions of these three very significant figures in the formation of African-American drama in the 1920s, we hear little about them in relation to this genre. Indeed, commentary today, in the form of books and essays, rarely moves away from Harlem and even more rarely makes any mention of the developing black stage during that decade. The designation of "Harlem Renaissance" for nearly all activity by black writers of this period illustrates how over-powering the influence of Harlem was and still is. Little acknowledged by historians and critics of that period is the quiet revolution that was going on in black little-theater groups. For a grasp of the impact of these three men on Richardson and on African-American drama in general during the 1920s, it is necessary to point out how whites shaped much black literature.

Nearly all discussions of American literature written during the 1920s turn, it seems, to what is called the Harlem Renaissance. Lasting approximately from the return of servicemen at the close of World War I to 1930 and the early years of the Depression—the dates vary among scholars—this period is noted for its vigorous production of work by African-American artists and writers. Works by Zora Neale Hurston, Jean Toomer, and Langston Hughes, among many other writers, have been documented and analyzed perhaps more than those works by black writers of any decade since. Yet to locate an authentic African-American voice, one must turn not only to what was written by blacks, but also to what was written for and published by blacks as well.

A photograph of a 1926 production by the Krigwa Little Theatre at the Harlem Library reveals an audience unlike that associated with Harlem, for it depicts a group of young people in home-made costumes standing on a low and simple stage.[1] It appears that the play has ended as black women, wearing winter coats and cloche hats, and black men, dressed in suits and ties, their shoes polished, applaud. More than simply capturing the people both on and off stage, the photograph draws attention to the rarely acknowledged and perhaps little-known fact that works other than musicals and cabaret shows were staged by blacks in Harlem. The photograph points this out and exposes the faulty interpretations and consequent misunderstandings that often accompany discussions of the Harlem Renaissance. Frequently forgotten is the fact that another Harlem existed, a Harlem that did not, and was not meant to, include whites. Such is the scene depicted in the photograph.

Images of Harlem during the 1920s do not usually include school-age children in homemade costumes or folding chairs for spectators. Instead, in looking through magazines and newspapers of that period, today's reader finds mention of light-skinned female dancers in feathered costumes, smiling black men crooning of the South, of "black and tan" cabarets, vaudeville shows in black face, of *Strut, Miss Lizzie* (1922), *Chocolate Dandies* (1924), and *Lucky Sambo* (1925). Between 1910 and 1940, more than 800 song-and-dance shows were produced that featured black performers. Through song and dance revues, plantation settings, and characters pining for the Old South, the African Americans who wrote for and played to a "Nordic" audience were reinforcing old stage caricatures. As black writer Sterling Brown noted in 1933, "One [image] is merely a jazzed up version of the other, with cabarets supplanting cabins, and Harlemized 'blues,' instead of spirituals and slave reels" (qtd. in Moses 119). Opinions of the early African-American stage based only on the musicals are necessarily incomplete: they overlook concurrent developments on other African-American stages at that time. The gaps and misreadings have reinforced the belief that African Americans working with the stage—either on or off—were writing for white tastes.

The perception of black people as uncivilized, as primitive, as inferior "others," was fueled by several "cultural moments." The publicity of Stanley and Livingston's meeting in Africa and the ensuing "scramble for Africa" in the latter part of the nineteenth century led to the 1907 Paris exhibition of African art.[2] By 1914, collecting African art had been popularized in works by Matisse and Picasso among others. The European interest in African art gave it a legitimacy and thereby stimulated interest in it among white collectors on this side of the Atlantic. Although the art of Africa was validated as "good" and collectible by European art critics and artists, it was, in the United States, transmuted into an extension and reinforcement of many stereotypes found on the minstrel stage. The interest in and curiosity about things African no doubt contributed to the immense popularity of President Theodore Roosevelt's book recounting his safari, *African Game Trail*, published in 1910, Edgar Rice Burroughs's *Tarzan of the Apes*, published in 1911, and Vachel Lindsay's 1915 poem "The Congo." These presentations of Africa and its people popularized the image of the peoples descended from the "dark continent" as primitive or savage at worst, and exotic at best.[3] Drawn from a non-European culture, artifacts and art forms exported from Africa were unfamiliar to white readers except through the white constructions by Lindsay, Burroughs, and others. Superstition, latent sexuality, and a sensuality seen as natural and unencumbered by puritanism appealed to white tastes in a nearly voyeuristic way. This view of Africa, an Africa imagined by whites, neatly fit the stereotype of blacks as less than civilized.

The literature often associated with the Harlem Renaissance was, to a large extent, made possible by white supporters. The interest of whites in black literature and art was perhaps the most important force in the evolution of the African-American writers who were part of the scene in Harlem. Among others, Hurston, Hughes, and Locke looked to the kindness of Charlotte Osgood Mason, a white benefactress and collector of Native American and African art. She demanded that these writers, as Bruce Kellner points out, "eschew subjects she judged as didactic or smacking of social reform" (Kellner, *Harlem* 97). As long as these artists lived up to (or down to) her image of what black art should be and artists should produce, they gained her financial graces. Although Mason's patronage made possible the development of several African-American writers who might otherwise have gone unnoticed, the sincerity of much of what was written under her financial support is questionable if one considers that it was written for white readers, published by white firms, reviewed by white columnists, and financed by a white American. Each writer was, as Nathan Huggins has noted, "the performer in a strange, almost macabre, act of black collusion in his own emasculation" (245).

Black writers affiliated with whites paid a price for the support they received. As James C. McKelly has noted,

The degree to which [minority] art receives its life-giving promotional attention and cultural exposure depends upon what the arbiters of commercial aesthetic culture estimate to be its potential acceptance in the dominant culture; yet to achieve this vital commercial acceptance, African-American art and literature had to abandon or thoroughly conceal, whatever qualities distinguish it as an authentic expression of minority experience in the first place. (89)

This abandonment by black writers resulted in a literature that was less powerful and less honest than it otherwise might have been. In effect, black literature often associated with Harlem is whitewashed. This is seen in the plays written about black life by both blacks and whites in the first decades of the century.

Whites did not doubt that black life was an untapped source for drama. Writers black and white pointed especially to the folk tradition as both the origin of the African-American voice and a fertile source for material. In *The New Negro* (1925), Locke, its editor, extolled the folk element as being the source for the real black voice in American literature. He hoped that through the development of the African-American folk tradition, black writers would produce their own literature. The folk tradition, the truly African-American voice of African-American theater in the early twentieth century, however, attracted the attention of many white playwrights in their search for new material. Indeed, Eugene O'Neill wrote to Gregory on this point: "The gifts the Negro can—and will—bring to our native drama are limitless and, to a dramatist, they open up new and intriguing opportunities. I have already written two plays on Negro life and plan to write more." As those involved in theater were well aware, and as Montgomery Gregory, the head of the Theater Department at Howard University, had correctly noted, "Paul Green, Ridgely Torrence, and Eugene O'Neill have done for us that which we ought to have done for ourselves."[4] The white playwrights had, Gregory pointed out, "shown that the ambitious dramatist has a rich and virgin El Dorado in the racial experiences of Black folk." To Gregory, "the only avenue of genuine achievement in American drama for the Negro lies in the development of the rich vein of folk tradition of the past and in the portrayal of the authentic life of the Negro masses of today" ("Native Drama" 159).

Throughout the decade, many whites encouraged African Americans to draw on their folk culture. In 1924, German director Max Reinhardt commented to Locke that African Americans should not even look to "the drama of the past, to the European drama." He pointed out that if there were to be a truly American form of drama, it would be African American. He urged Locke, who was by that time working with the Howard Players, to "be original—sense the folk spirit, develop . . . the folk-idiom"[5] The survey "The Negro in Art: How Shall He Be Portrayed?," which was published in *Crisis* from February through October in 1926, sought opinions from black and white writers about the state of black literature. Eugene O'Neill, a respondent, urged blacks to "write about what you [know]" (Letter 17). Carl Van Vechten remarked that there would "never be a truly Negro theatre until it is founded on racial heritage" ("Uncle Tom" 62).

In 1922, Carter Woodson sought the development of black drama in his call for blacks to write their own literature: "We should develop a literature. Negroes should read some things written by their own people that they may be inspired thereby. . . . We must cease trying to straighten our hair and bleach our faces, and be Negroes—and be good ones" ("Some Things" 34).

O'Neill voiced similar sentiments in 1925:

I have read a good number of plays written by Negroes and they were always *bad* plays . . . *unoriginal—and what revolted me the most, bad imitations in method and thought of conventional white plays!* . . . Be yourselves! Don't reach out for *our* stuff which *we* call good! Make your own stuff and your good!" (Letter 17–18)

Locke pointed out that "white dramatists like O'Neill and [Earnest] Culbertson . . . come to race material as explorers, not as familiars." He believed that a "fine development of race drama will require intimate knowledge of the folk life and folk temperament" and that a consciousness of the folk element would "come in large measure from the Negro dramatist." In his Drama Notes, as yet unpublished, Locke wrote that it was a question, "not of race but of intimate understanding." O'Neill, Torrence, and their successors did not, could not, write from experience; the stage works that they produced were, according to theater historian James V. Hatch, "synthetic folk plays, seeking the exotic Negro rather than the real Afro-American—a being whom whites had no way of knowing" ("A White Folks Guide" 4).

In a circuitous manner, Mabel Dodge, in gatherings at her home in Greenwich Village, influenced several whites who would later write folk plays on black life. In 1912, ten years earlier than Mason, Dodge, a wealthy white woman, formed a salon of white intellectuals and writers. Her gatherings afforded those attending them the time and space to discuss African-American culture and to explore—some might say exploit—how this topic might be tapped by their own pens.[6] Although Dodge is not known to have funded any black artists or writers, as had Mason, her salon is important in discussions of early African-American drama. Several of those who assembled there later supported or wrote various interpretations of African-American culture: Ridgely Torrence, who wrote *Three Plays for a Negro Theater*; Emilie Hapgood, who backed Torrence's production and funded the Hapgood Players, a black theater group; Paul Green, who based several of his plays on African-American folk culture; Dorothy and DuBose Heyward, who collaborated on the play based on her novel *Porgy*; and Michael Gold, whose 1930 play *Hoboken Blues* was called the black *Rip Van Winkle*.

Sponge-like, Harlem has absorbed nearly all scholarly attention paid to the 1920s. Preoccupation with the black writers in that location has deflected attention from other areas—both geographic and literary—of that same period. As a result, artistic developments by African Americans, especially by black dramatists, outside of this small pocket in New York have been, for the most part, relatively neglected. No doubt, the very label for that period—the Harlem Renaissance—has been part of the reason for an incomplete understanding of the decade and a lack of full and deserving attention paid to other geographic areas. African Americans were writing "good literature" in other parts of the United States: in Chicago and Cleveland and along the East Coast in Boston, Philadelphia, Baltimore, and Washington, D.C. An alternate and, arguably, more accurate view of black culture during the 1920s, a view not tarnished by the involvement of white publishers, promoters, and entrepreneurs, is found in the work of African-American playwrights who wrote for black audiences.

In claiming a place on the American stage, African-American playwrights drew on materials with which they were familiar—the folk culture. During the 1920s, Richardson and other black playwrights presented the African-American experience quite differently than that seen in black folk plays written by whites. In doing so, they prepared the way for today's African-American playwrights. The audience and actors described at the beginning of this chapter are important because they are the intended and immediate recipients—indeed, one might say, first informed "reviewers"—of African-American drama in the first three decades of the twentieth century. Beyond Harlem and its denizens, the folk drama grew as an artistic form. Rooted in the slavery of the Deep South, African-American folk drama took its shape on little-theater stages.

An alternate label for the Harlem Renaissance is "New Negro Renaissance," a designation this period is also given, which more accurately reflects the emergence of confidence among blacks seen in other areas of the country. Changes in self-perception were reflected in materials viewed in less public surroundings than Harlem. A new estimation of the race by African Americans bloomed, to a great extent, through the works of the black dramatists in the black little-theater organizations. Indeed, a revolution was going on in the meeting rooms of black churches, in the basements of public libraries, and in the auditoriums of black colleges and schools throughout much of the United States. It was in and through the work of the drama groups, mostly sponsored by schools, churches, and community organizations—and not in the flash and adventure of the Harlem writers—that the story of Africans in America was learned, recorded, and enacted. In a sense, the African-American little-theater groups were part of an underground movement in that their works, unlike those by writers of the Harlem Renaissance, were never part of the mainstream or, as black writer Haki Madhubuti has called it, "whitestream" culture, nor were they intended to be. Instead, the plays produced by little-theater groups were attempts both to preserve the African-American folk tradition and to educate and thereby empower African-American audiences.

It has been suggested that the African-American dramatists of that period were competing with white playwrights. These critics contend that through the stage, black playwrights hoped to undermine the images of African Americans seen on the white stage. This is partly true, for surely "if true black characters could be portrayed on stage, the old Negro stereotypes could be driven off the boards" (Hatch, "White" 210). The African Americans writing for little-theater groups were not, however, competing directly with the white stage. The audiences for popular stage shows and for plays written for and performed by little-theater groups were different.

In holding their plays in churches and similar locations and in basing their plays on topics relevant to the lives of blacks—lynching, passing, and the migration north, for example—the little-theater groups were obviously *not* trying to change the images whites held of blacks, for African Americans knew that the stereotypes were incorrect. The African-American audience was the chief reason for their writing at all, not for white dollars or white recognition with a price tag.

African Americans in general had a different purpose in writing their plays from that of their white counterparts. Black American poet-dramatist Melvin Dixon, addressing this difference in 1969, noted that the "common quest" of black theater was for a "total liberation," one "free at last from the rusty chains of Western aesthetics" (42). In their plays, the dramatists affirmed the African-American community by acknowledging it. The plays raised topics of urgent and real concern to a minority audience: African-American soldiers serving in Europe for a country that had not outlawed lynching, the need for the distribution of birth control information, the crusade for women's suffrage. One could say that nearly all early African-American plays, similar to many written today, had a message, an ostensible purpose. Unlike the plays on black life written by white dramatists during that decade, these plays were not written to entertain. The versions of "Negro life" popular with white audiences were written, generally, in the conventions expected by and with the stereotypes acceptable to white audiences and producers. The plots and conflicts developed by the black playwrights for the little-theater movement were quite different; African-American dramatists, for the most part, wrote from their own experiences of being black in white America.

At literary gatherings and in the pages of black magazines, to which Richardson was a contributor, African-American writers raised several questions regarding the development of African-American drama: What should be the purpose of the African-American stage—to entertain or to educate? What topics would appeal to black urban playgoers? Should race issues necessarily be a part of black plays? Who was the intended audience? Did dialect have a place on the black stage, or did it set back the progress of the race through its associations with minstrelsy and slavery? Where would African-American playwrights be found? Television and films have made several of these questions—that of audience, for example—moot today. During the 1920s, however, they disturbed black writers. Together, the early black playwrights battled the Goliath of the white stage and its representations of black life. In his *Souls of Black Folk*, Du Bois addressed one obstacle the early black playwrights had to contend with in his frequently quoted passage on "double-consciousness." He wrote of the contortions an African American went through in "looking at one's self through the eyes of others"(5). Ever operating in a duality, ever wearing the mask about which Paul Laurence Dunbar had written in his poem "We Wear the Mask" (1893), many African-American writers had to shape their work to suit a double audience. In 1928, James Weldon Johnson remarked on this same dilemma faced by an African-American writer:

> To whom shall he address himself, to his own Black group or to white America? Many a Negro writer has fallen down . . . between these two stools. . . . It is doubtful if anything with meaning can be written unless the writer has some definite audience in mind. ("Dilemma" 93)

As members of a minority race, African Americans found that when dealing with whites, survival—both actual and internal—was more assured if contrary ways and contentious thoughts were squelched. Acting "uppity" or stepping out of line would only further confound the delicate relationship between the races in the United States, a relationship in which blacks had little bargaining power.

In the same year that Johnson's remarks were published, the writer of a manual on minstrelsy confirmed the dualities on which both Johnson and Du Bois had written. In *Gentlemen, Be Seated*, white author Gerald Paskman acknowledged that to the African American "white minstrel[sy] owes everything, for without the presence of the black race in this country American minstrelsy would never have existed." Blacks have given, he noted, "the richest material for translation for the stage" (176). In closing his book of song lyrics, the position of the players on stage, and information on how to apply blackface makeup, Paskman reassured his readers that the guidebook was *not* "presented as an obituary to minstrelsy, but as an advance notice of its *permanent* life" (italics added) (240).

Richardson and other early black playwrights addressed the twin issues of writing for a double audience and of writing against prevailing stereotypes that they wanted to bury and for which they wanted to write "an obituary."[7] Black playwrights sought to change the images that had accumulated by the 1920s—lingering elements of the nineteenth-century stage then popularized by the hundreds of vaudeville shows and musical revues. In a very real way, Richardson and his contemporaries were iconoclasts, who challenged and tried to smash the stage images that had been in place, both on stage and off, for more than a century.

The early black playwrights could assume that a black audience was familiar with the reality of these problems, with the difficulties of adapting to life in cities, with discrimination based on mixed blood, and with poverty. From the outset, many playwrights had an audience that did not need to be educated about its shared hardships; they had only to be brought together through the community of a production. As African-American critic Abena Busia points out,

By giving ourselves a voice through our literature, we introduce into the masquerade of the traditional Western literary canon the dialogue we insist upon. . . . Our writers do not simply rewrite or recreate literature of the ruling class in Black face, but strive for something "other." (15–16)

Through the stage, the pioneer playwrights attempted to define this "other." As those who had experienced slavery had also written about it, African-American dramatists were writing their own interpretation of American history. However, rather than have it filtered by white editors, as many slave narratives had been, the playwrights sought a form that was based on their own cultural experiences and plots that included enslavement, lynching, and continual prejudice. Unlike the antebellum slave narratives, which were largely sponsored by, written for, and published by white sympathizers, the plays for the African-American dramatic stage were written by and for African Americans.

By staying within the black community and by writing for it, black dramatists relinquished the fame or popularity that their works might have had if they had been written for white producers and publishers and, by extension, white audiences and readers. By not directing their plays to whites, those early black dramatists are, consequently, relatively unknown today. Yet the African-American tradition in today's theater, the one to which Dixon alludes, was established by those black American playwrights who persevered, uncompromisingly, despite the packed theaters holding song and dance shows and despite the interpretations of black culture popularized by white dramatists of the day. The folk element, a defining feature of most early African-American drama, was drawn from the lives and experiences of men and women whose grandparents, and perhaps parents, had more than likely been slaves. One could say that their "children" recorded their stories in their plays. The African-American dramatists of the 1920s related more authentically African-American life and culture than works written *by* whites *about* blacks could possibly have done. Whites did not, indeed could not, participate in the creation of African-American drama based on such experiences.

Although not necessarily based on the experiences of the playwrights themselves, elements of the plays were part of a heritage common to both playwrights and viewers. The plots, characters, incidents, and dialect were familiar to a black audience, whether that audience sat in the auditorium of a black school or in the basement of a library or in the assembly room of a church. In writing for that audience, these playwrights were freed from the strictures set by white theater organizations, white audiences, and, for the most part, white publishing houses. Untroubled by the dilemma of the double audience about which Johnson had written in 1928, black playwrights were able to write freely, for they knew their audience and their material. There was an understanding and a familiarity between playwright and spectator about the material presented, for outside of the theater, both lived in a culture dominated by whites.

In their plays, the early black dramatists most often focused on the well-being of a community, whether it was a family, a neighborhood, or the race in general. Through themes of social and political oppression of African Americans, the plays nearly always had a purpose greater than entertainment as they addressed racial issues, taught black history, bolstered the morale of the audience, and explored situations and problems within the black community.

Reaped from the soil of slavery, the folk tradition distinguished African-American plays from those derived from a European aesthetic and tradition; the folk tradition was part of black culture, it had survived on the plantations, and it had traveled north to the cities where it was kept alive through the black church and community. Plays derived from the folk culture were a form of black nationalism in that they neither borrowed from white culture nor were written for a white audience. Folk drama looked at life directly by including the raw materials of poverty and ignorance. Without attempting to satisfy white tastes and expectations and without the veneer of gentility that earlier black playwrights had used, folk plays presented a reality not present in the plays on black life written by whites at that time, a reality largely absent or glossed over in the few plays written by African Americans in the nineteenth century. Slavery, the folk culture of the rural South, and the migration to the industrial North had shaped African-American culture. Questions of defining the audience or finding a suitable subject for the stage became immaterial when black dramatists directed their energies toward developing, preserving, and writing from the folk tradition for black audiences. It was in the folk tradition that African-American drama found its voice.

The little-theater movement became the most valuable force in organizing the black folk theater and in solving some of its difficulties. As Bruce Kellner has pointed out, "Fearing the death of the Afro-American folk play because of the popularity of the black Broadway revues, Du Bois organized a 'little Negro theatre' through the *Crisis*" (*Harlem* 212). These theater organizations were, in effect, laboratories for community-based productions, a venue urged by Du Bois. The true black theater tradition originated and was first tested in these locations. More than 470 black little-theater groups were founded between 1910 and 1930. Chief among these was Krigwa, an acronym for *Crisis* Guild of Writers and Artists. Organized by Du Bois, Zora Neale Hurston and others, Krigwa theater groups, active from 1926 through 1935, were formed in New York, Philadelphia, Baltimore, Washington, D.C., and other East Coast cities. In his notes, Locke mentions such other African-American little-theater groups as the Scribblers of Baltimore, the Dixwell Players of New Haven, the Gilpins of Cleveland, the Quill Club of Boston, the Shadows of Chicago, as well as groups in Dallas, Philadelphia, and Indianapolis (Drama Notes). Little known is that Marcus Garvey's United Negro Improvement Association too had a drama group; located in Harlem, it produced plays written by Garvey and others.[8]

Du Bois understood that "with the growth of . . . colored theaters, a new demand for Negro drama has arisen which is only partially satisfied by the vaudeville actors." Du Bois was aware of the resistance white theater owners would have to producing serious plays by African Americans: "If it is a Negro play that will interest us and depict our life, experience and humor, it cannot be sold to the ordinary theatrical producer." He urged, instead, that plays written by African Americans be "produced in our churches, and lodges, and halls" ("Paying for Plays" 7–8). Black churches sponsored youth theater groups, and their congregations produced plays and pageants based on figures from black history and the Bible. Black schools formed drama clubs, and neighborhood created drama organizations. The simple dramas portrayed aspects of black history, such as slavery and rebellion, as well as topics of more immediate concern to African Americans. In a sense, most of the plays were morality tales wrapped inside one-act dramas. Written as allegories, these presentations were known as race dramas or problem plays, for they most commonly addressed the difficult situations with which African Americans contended.

Rather than mask the actual lives of blacks, African-American plays written in the early 1920s for black audiences mirrored black problems and dealt with them head on. The characters are generally indigent and uneducated, and dialect is frequently spoken. Absent are the retread stereotypes from the white stage. One act long, the plays are usually set in rural southern areas or the characters have a tie to that region. Maya Angelou's comment that "all African Americans find their roots in the South" goes toward explaining why nearly all plays written by African Americans in the early twentieth century are connected to the South. Whether a family was emigrating from it and leaving behind their kinfolk, visiting relatives who still lived there, attempting to return, or longing for it, the South is knit into the fabric of these plays.

Generally, the race plays included highly dramatic elements. Poverty, miscegenation, passing (with its inevitable tragedy), and lynching were common topics. These aspects of black America's past, however, were, in a sense, embraced by the playwrights, for they depicted what African Americans had survived and still battled. In a sense, the forbearance of the protagonist and his or her community was not only a distinguishing feature of black folk plays but a point of pride, an indication of the race's strength. In drawing from their heritage, the early black playwrights acknowledged the links of African Americans everywhere—even those who disavowed such connections—to the folk tradition culturally, spiritually, historically, emotionally, and socially. The migration north was not a distant memory for many of the audience members who sat in church basements watching John Matheus's play 'Cruiter or Joseph Mitchell's *Help Wanted*. Nor was the situation in Georgia Johnson's play on lynching, *A Sunday Morning in the South*, necessarily fiction. Having migrated from Georgia and the Carolinas, many audience members could relate to the hardships told of in plots set in the rural South and to the consequent damage done to black families and culture by leaving those familiar locales for the industrial North.

Another common feature of many early black plays is the inclusion of white characters as the force that opposes or undermines the success, livelihood, and, frequently, lives of black characters. They were prey to whites in any number of situations represented on stage: victimized or lynched by white gangs, forced to be breeders, ensnared by white landlords, discriminated against after moving to "the Promised Land" in northern cities, or abused by their white employers. In these respects, the plays are obvious precursors to Hansberry's *A Raisin in the Sun*.[9]

Nearly always grim, the endings of these early black problem plays usually include either the death of a main character or the prospect of a bleak future. Mary Burrill's play *Aftermath* (1918), for example, tells of a decorated black serviceman's return from the war in Europe to his southern home to find that his father has only recently been lynched by a white gang. In Georgia Johnson's play *A Sunday Morning in the South* (1925), an innocent young black man is taken from his family on a Sunday morning and hanged by a white mob that suspects him of flirting with a white woman. Myrtle Livingston Smith's *For Unborn Children* (1926) concerns the decisions a young man must make who is engaged to a white woman. Although he loves her, he breaks off the affair so that his unborn children will not have to face mixed parentage, as he did. At the end of the play, he exits his cabin, leaving behind his grandmother and sister, and offers himself to the waiting lynch mob. Johnson's *Plumes* (1927) features a mother who must choose between giving her ill child the remote chance of surviving an illness or putting that money into a grand funeral, complete with plumed horses, for her daughter. In Marita Bonner's *The Pot Maker* (1927) a black man is killed by his wife for his emotional battering of her. In Johnson's play *Safe* (1929), a black mother gives thanks for her infant's death, for it precludes the possibility of his ever being lynched by whites. Bonner's *The Purple Flower* (1928), an expressionistic play, virulently condemns the "white devils."[10]

Although their work has received even less attention than that of women, several African-American men wrote folk plays during the 1920s.[11] Like those of their female counterparts, the plays by men are often set in the South and end with a death. Again, whites are cast as antagonists. In the plays by black men, however, white characters, who are nearly always male, undermine the male protagonist's manhood and his power over his own life. Much more frequently than the plays by women, the plays by men often include a male-female relationship and a sexual aspect. In G. D. Lipscomb's play *Frances* (1925), for example, the father of a young black woman coerces her into a sexual relationship with the white foreman. Set in the antebellum South, Randolph Edmonds' *Breeders* (1930) concerns a black woman whose master attempts to force her to have intercourse with a black man in order to produce strong slave children; rather than submit, she poisons herself. In *Ti Yette* (1930), by John Matheus, a young woman is torn between her love for a white man and her African heritage, which her brother accuses her of forsaking. By the play's end, her brother murders her rather than let Ti Yette marry her white lover. Jean Toomer's *Balo, A Sketch of Negro Life* (1922) is an example of a play unlike those by other black playwrights of this decade. First performed by the Howard Players in 1923, the play, set among black sharecroppers in Georgia, focuses on the religious experience of a young black man.[12]

Male playwrights also frequently focused on a white antagonist's efforts to thwart the black male character from succeeding or even holding a job. In the folk plays, black employees are discriminated against by white foremen, and unsuspecting black men are cheated out of wages by whites. More often than those by women, the plays by African-American men often include the migration north in order to earn a decent wage. Their plays often focus on the consequences such a move has on the black family as it adapts to life far from its roots. The plot of Matheus's *'Cruiter* (1926) centers on a white recruiter from Detroit who, with the promise of a better life, lures a young black couple to work in a factory there; their departure, however, brings about the death of the husband's grandmother, who has been left behind in the South. Joseph Mitchell's *Help Wanted* (1929) similarly shows the difficulties brought about by whites when a black couple moves to Chicago in search of a better life. The male protagonist is cheated out of receiving credit for a money-saving invention. In Edmonds's *Old Man Pete* (1930), an elderly married couple sells the family home in Virginia to live with their children in New York City. Embarrassed by the folk ways and dialect of their parents, the children, in a plot that is akin to *King Lear*, banish their elderly parents. Rather than humiliate their children, they leave for Virginia and are found frozen to death on a park bench.

Whether set in the North or South, the plays of both men and women frequently center on characters who are caught in the nets of post-Emancipation slavery. In many of these plays, the North is presented not as the golden or "Promised Land" that Matheus's white job recruiter holds out to lure the young couple to Detroit. Instead, the North is presented both as a location destructive to folk culture and the black family and as a place where slavery under whites continues to thrive, albeit in a different guise. Plays set in the South present an equally unfavorable life for African-American families, as it is shown to be deeply entrenched in the subtle slavery of peonage and sharecropping and the on-going gross abuse of blacks.

In an essay published in 1922, Locke wrote that if African Americans would only "till the native soil of the race life" they would see that they had a "peculiar natural endowment" for the stage ("Steps" 66). By 1922, Locke, along with Montgomery Gregory, had begun setting up a theater department at Howard University for which students were writing plays. That same year, Mary Burrill introduced Richardson to Locke, who saw Richardson as a playwright of promise for the black stage. Locke was confident that through the stage, he could substantiate his claim that African Americans had a heritage worth preserving, one that was not in competition with but rather distinct from work by white writers.

Locke and Du Bois agreed on the importance of developing the folk drama: it was the purpose and plots of the plays, however, on which the two men disagreed. To Locke, "the flower of Negro drama [would] probably be the folk play rather than the problem play. It will express beautifully the folk life of the race and beautify its nature." It would, he hoped, later move to "a poetic and somewhat symbolic style of drama that will remind us of Synge and the Irish folk theater or the Yiddish theater" (Drama Notes).

Du Bois and Locke debated the purpose of African-American drama. For Locke, the stage was a means of entertaining an audience, whether black or white, and of preserving African-American folk culture, as his unpublished notes on drama reveal: "With the spread of Black drama," he wrote, "the provinces are waking up and a new cult of beauty stirs almost throughout the land." Locke was adamantly opposed to "race" plays, those that spoke to an oppressed minority and poised blacks against whites. Since the early part of the century, African-American drama had, Locke pointed out, taken one of two courses, both derived from *Uncle Tom's Cabin*. It had either followed Topsy and taken its place on the vaudeville stage to be laughed at, or it had been "infected" by Uncle Tom and drenched itself in the "plague" of "propagandistic sentimentalities" and "maudlin moralizing." These "artistically futile efforts" at problem plays, all written by "amateur Negroes," were, in Locke's opinion, "legion" (Drama Notes). He believed, instead, that folk plays should avoid protest and problems and focus on realism and "more purely aesthetic attitudes."

For the sake of freer, clearer artistic expression, we must retrieve the native optimism and joy of living and leave more and more to the exploitation of those dramatists not born to it the dramatization of the problem. We must concern ourselves more vitally with it as life: we cannot afford to anatomize and dissect, we must paint; we must create. (Drama Notes)[13]

Among the several writers who sided with Locke was Eulalie Spence, a playwright and occasional columnist for *Opportunity*: "May I advise those earnest few—those seekers after light—white lights—to avoid the drama of propaganda if they would not meet with certain disaster. The white man is cold and unresponsive to this subject and the Negro. . . . We go to the theatre for entertainment" (180). Cofounder and manager of the Gilpin Players, the theater group of the Karamu House in Cleveland, Rowena Jelliffe, a white, agreed: "The theater should not be considered a medium for propaganda. Undue concern about putting the best racial foot forward should be forgot" ("Gilpin" 344).[14]

Du Bois had differing views of propaganda. African-American drama should serve a purpose, whether that lay in joining people together, in portraying black history, in confronting issues of oppression, or in raising the morale of the audience. The most democratic of genres, the stage gathered a black audience together in the community of a shared event. Even illiteracy did not interfere with understanding a play. As critic Rollin Lynde Hartt had noted, "Throughout Black America . . . Negroes, unable to read, see Negro plays performed by Negroes in establishments owned and managed by Negroes" (161).

In providing a literal and figurative platform for showing problematic situations and their solutions, drama didn't rely on literacy to be understood by or to affect an audience. Further, because drama is a visual art, the figures from black history and life who walked the boards were, in a sense, made real to those who may have had little sense of black history. To Du Bois, these features made the stage too forceful a medium and invested it with an energy too valuable to a newly freed population to be spent on frivolous entertainment and Locke's "new cult of beauty," "native optimism," or "joy of living."

Through *Crisis*, Du Bois had promoted the use of the stage for propaganda purposes. He himself had used it in this manner with his own pageant "The Star of Ethiopia" (1915). The most vocal proponent of black drama in the early part of the century, in 1926 he wrote, "We do not believe in any art simply for art's sake." Several months later he was bolder, stating in an editorial, "I do not care a damn for any art that is not propaganda."[15] Poet and columnist Countee Cullen agreed, writing that it was "bad counsel to advise Negroes to refrain from anything that smacks of propaganda [that is, education]." He urged playwrights not to "threw [sic] away the Negro dialect, to abandon materials of Negro life—in short to forget he is a Negro" (180). To black feminist, writer, and educator

Anna Julia Cooper, the difference between drama used to inform and drama used to entertain was not clear. As she wrote to Locke, "Tell us just what constitutes race drama and how we may know it when we find it."[16]

During the 1920s, the most active decade of his career, Richardson wrote his seven most widely produced plays: *The Chip Woman's Fortune* (1923), *The Broken Banjo* (1925), *The Bootblack Lover* (1926), *Compromise* (1926), *The Flight of the Natives* (1927), *The House of Sham* (1929), and *The Idle Head* (1929). He also wrote six essays, published between November 1919 and September 1925, in which he stated his views of and visions for the black theater. Those short articles focus chiefly on two of Richardson's ongoing concerns: the use of the stage as a means of educating an African-American audience; and the types of characters and topics toward which African-American playwrights should direct their energy. To Richardson, the purpose and the plot were inseparably intertwined.

As will be discussed, the types of characters he created and the dilemmas with which they contend set his work apart from that of his colleagues. In the very areas that made their plays so similar to one another—the tensions between whites and blacks and their frequent reliance on melodrama—Richardson differed. To him, black drama should focus on the black community itself. The problems and situations there, he believed, supplied enough drama without the interference of white characters. Through his distinctive contributions to the African-American stage via the folk drama, Richardson is considered by some scholars to be the father of African-American folk drama. Like his nearly spiritual mentor Du Bois, Richardson believed strongly in the use of the stage as a platform for educating black audiences. By enacting problematic situations on stage, he hoped not only to portray "ordinary people," but also to teach blacks the necessity of working together.

NOTES

1. The caption under the photograph identifies the location as the "Playhouse of the Little Negro Theatre, Harlem, New York City." Bernard L. Peterson, Jr., has identified the Krigwa Players as the drama group. This photograph appeared in *Crisis* in July 1926, p. 135.

2. For a discussion of the influence of Africa on Western culture, see Jan Nederveen Pieterse, *White on Black: Images of Africa and Blacks in Western Popular Culture*. New Haven: Yale UP, 1992. pp. 183–90.

3. See Chapter 1, "New Views on Old Prejudices," 3–44, in Chidi Ikonne, *From Du Bois to Van Vechten: The Early New Negro Literature, 1903–1926*. Westport, CT: Greenwood Press, 1981.

4. See "Native Drama" in *Plays of Negro Life: A Source-Book of Native American Drama*. Ed. Alain Locke [1927]. New York: Negro UP, 1968. p. 122.

5. Quoted in Locke, "Max Rheinhardt [sic] Reads the Negro's Dramatic Horoscope." *Opportunity* 2 (May 1924): pp. 145–46.

6. For a discussion of Mabel Dodge's salon, see Harold Cruse *The Crisis of the Negro Intellectual: A Historical Analysis of the Failure of Black Leadership*. New York: Quill, 1984. 22–32.

7. This death notice was dramatized on stage in 1932 in an obscure play written by Arthur Clifton Lamb of Morgan State College in Baltimore. Named *Shades of Cotton Lips* for the whiteness of a minstrel player's lips, the unpublished play centers on the trial of a minstrel character. Found guilty by a black jury of holding back the race, he is permanently banished from the black stage. A similar situation is found in *The Trial and Banishment of Uncle Tom* (1945), in which Uncle Tom is found guilty for his crime of perpetuating black stage stereotypes. Randolph Edmonds, the playwright, played the role of the judge. Unfortunately, this play has not been located and no bibliographic information is available.

8. See ch. 6 in Tony Martin, *Literary Garveyism: Garvey, Black Arts and the Harlem Renaissance*. Dover, MA: Majority Press, 1983.

9. During the 1920s, African-American folk plays were seldom written in a light vein. Only three comedies produced by little-theater groups are known to this writer: *The Church Fight* (1925) by Ruth Shelton Gaines, *The Yellow Peril* (1925) George Schuyler, and *Riding the Goat* (1930) by May Miller.

10. Barbara Molette believes that Amiri Baraka may have been familiar with *The Purple Flower* and used it as a model for several of his own plays (Interview).

11. According to Elizabeth Brown-Guillory, the "burst of dramatic creativity [during the 1920s] is associated solely with Black male playwrights" (*Their Place* 3). This claim would, however, be difficult to substantiate. In fact, very little scholarship has been done on works by male playwrights of that decade. Brown-Guillory may, however, be mixing musicals with non-musical works. The attention scholars have paid to non-musical plays by African Americans during the 1920s has focused largely on plays by women.

12. *Kabnis* (1923), the last section of Toomer's novel *Cane*, has a setting similar to *Balo*. An interesting note to these two plays is that Toomer thought *Kabnis* the better play and wanted Locke to include it in *Plays of Negro Life*; Locke would not allow it, insisting that *Balo* portrayed the African-American folk more accurately.

13. Curiously, notes in Locke's hand are often identical to those published under Gregory's name in the essay "The Drama of Negro Life" in *The New Negro*. Compare, for example, Locke's "Topsy has given us a fearful progeny" with Gregory's identical comment on page 155 of *The New Negro*.

14. That *Opportunity*, the publication of the Urban League, was intended for both black and white readers and that *Crisis* was directed primarily toward blacks no doubt affected the views of Charles S. Johnson and Du Bois, the respective editors.

15. See "Krigwa, 1926," *Crisis* (Jan. 1926): p. 115, and "Criteria of Negro Art," *Crisis* (Oct. 1926): pp. 290–97.

16. Cooper's postcard to Locke invited him to speak to an unnamed group on Sunday, 12 May; no year was given. Cooper's return address at the time was 1630 Tenth Street in Washington, D.C.. Cooper was the "Directress" of the Washington, D.C., Dramatic Club, which was organized on 1 March 1912 to present "annually some play of classical rank" (Montgomery Gregory papers).

3

The Education of African Americans: Willis Richardson's Approach to Drama

> That the productions of [Negro] writers should have been some-
> thing of a guide in their daily living is a matter which never
> seems to have been raised seriously.
> —Richard Wright

In his 1937 essay "Blueprint for Negro Writing," Richard Wright discusses black writers who "dressed in the knee-pants of servility" as they went "abegging to white America" for approval. He notes that "Negro writing was something external to the lives of educated Negroes themselves" (394–95). Nearly twenty years earlier, Richardson was working to make "Negro writing" relevant to the lives of African Americans through his plays. In 1926, Du Bois wrote passionately about the stage in his call for black drama that would be "for us, by us, about us, and near us." Although he never identified whom his broad use of "us" represented, it is safe to assume that Du Bois was referring to those who found little to which they could relate in nearly any dramatic production at that time. Although Georgia Johnson, May Miller, and other black dramatists heeded Du Bois's call in most respects in their plays, Richardson followed a very different direction regarding "about us." In other plays of the 1920s, the "about us" aspect of African-American plays could actually be read as "about us and whites." White characters, it seems, were a necessary element in most early African-American plays. Richardson avoided relying on white characters in his plays, which may partly explain today's neglect of his work. That is, because his plays do not deal with racial strife, they seem not to have stirred interest among those researching African-American drama of the early twentieth century.

Although other black playwrights of the period wrote on topics pertinent to black life, few playwrights aside from Richardson sought material for their plays from within the black community and addressed the situations found there. In focusing on topics about and relevant to African Americans, the playwright had, by 1919, both addressed Wright's remarks in that Richardson's plays did not go "abegging to white America" for approval, and followed Du Bois's prescribed features for African-American drama.

Through this shift from the usual black-white tension, Richardson avoided the image of blacks as victimized by whites; consequently, white characters and white culture do not control his stage. In their reliance on whites as antagonists, his contemporaries, by continually giving power to white characters, acknowledged the control whites had over blacks, which resulted in the simplistic situation of "white is bad" and "black is good." The predictability of the outcome for a black character in a black-white conflict lessened the play's impact and its drama, for if white characters were present, a black spectator knew that the black characters were going to suffer at the hands of the whites. The results of Richardson's creating, instead, black-black tensions and conflicts, are rounded, three-dimensional characters, a feature rarely seen in African-American drama during its formative years.

Although *Rachel* had given him the impetus to write for the stage, "Miss Grimké's *Rachel*," he wrote, was "still not the thing [he] meant," for it "shows the manner in which Negroes are treated by white people in the United States" ("Hope" 338). The choices and decisions made on Richardson's stage are created and controlled by his black characters. By exploring situations and conditions within the black community, Richardson hoped to show his audiences that many of their problems and difficulties did not necessarily spring from encounters with whites, as Grimké's *Rachel* and plays by many of Richardson's contemporaries imply.

The difference between Richardson's works and plays by most of his contemporaries is evident when one considers other African-American plays written in the 1920s. Plays written by black women in the first decades of the century are, for example, frequently similar to one another. Although they implicitly attacked such stereotypical stage props as banjos and watermelons, they unwittingly created new stereotypes. Many of the folk plays written before 1930—especially those by women—feature the long-suffering, indigent black woman, the beleaguered African-American family, or the young black man about to be hanged. Churches and modest homes replace graveyards and plantations as a new cliché. Conflicts are frequently created around the impending lynching of a father or son or the encroachment of whites on the security of the black community. Georgia Johnson's *A Sunday Morning in the South* (1925) and *Safe* (1929), Mary Burrill's *Aftermath* (1919), and Myrtle Livingston Smith's *For Unborn Children* (1926), as examples, are strikingly similar in these respects.[1] Plays of this sort were no doubt the ones that Locke had in mind when he wrote about the "numerous Negro writers of amateur plays where [the] chief dramatic intention has been . . . moral allegories, rhetorical melodramas, and dramatic antidotes for race prejudice." Of Mary Burrill's play, for example, Locke wrote, "*They That Sit in the Dark* [sic] is written too obviously to point to a moral" (Drama Notes). The plots continually go beyond the black community in relying on whites as antagonists. In many of these plays, it seems that tensions among African Americans come about only when white characters are in the vicinity. Nearly always condemned for their victimization of blacks, whites are held responsible for the problems of the black community.[2]

Another common feature in the early black plays are the poverty-stricken characters. Because they are such a usual feature in these plays, they too create almost a stereotype of blacks. It is not that they are poor, however; instead, it is that they are spared feelings of malice or ill will. They are depicted, as Richardson wrote, as "angels," perhaps because they haven't been tainted by wealth, material goods, or life in the North. Presented as victims of circumstance, black characters are frequently predictable and, consequently, two-dimensional, nearly stock characters. This underprivileged class, the blacks, is often victimized by whites in power or with money. These plays are, for the most part, formulaic: a poor black family is preyed upon by cruel and selfish whites; the family suffers at the hands of whites; an African American is killed or dies because of whites. If these plays were designed to teach, one can only wonder what the lesson might have been. Such plays could only, one might surmise, increase tension between the races.

Richardson's plays reveal his belief that an individual sense of identity and self-worth must accompany any social reform. Attacks on white power meant that whites had a psychic and emotional hold or control over blacks. Placing whites as pivotal characters acknowledged their power, while deflecting attention from the strength and intelligence of blacks. In differentiating the black stage from the white stage, Carlton and Barbara Molette point to "purpose" as being an integral aspect of black drama:

The African (and Afro-American) concept of art is that art is inextricably connected to life. Art is supposed to be useful to society in contrast to the Eurocentric elitist art-for-art's sake tradition. . . . A black playwright [should] intentionally disseminate information that helps black people control their own lives, for their own betterment, on their own terms. (*Black Theater* 38)

Protest plays, such as those written by Richardson's colleagues, validated the structures of oppression. In Richardson's plays, the tension springs from the family and displays the effect on the black community when blacks themselves do not work together. Rather than attacking the white power structure, his plays have characters who deal with their own weaknesses and look to themselves as sources of strength. The white community is nearly absolved of its responsibility. His plays portray the essence of black experience in America by examining tensions between men and women, young and old, rich and poor, all set against the backdrop of urban life, rural settings, migrating north, and the church. Although the plays by women addressed matters of real concern to black Americans, these concerns become trivial through the plays' predictable reliance on melodrama. In emigrating from the South, blacks left behind their spiritual homes and entered a foreign land, a world unfamiliar and strange and one that they were often ill-equipped to handle socially, spiritually, or emotionally. By avoiding these extremes—the martyrs in plays by blacks and the exotic, dangerous or childlike in plays by whites—and by including "unpleasant endings," Richardson shifted his concerns to domestic situations, which he believed were more immediate and pressing to African Americans as they adapted to urban life.

In focusing on black-on-black relations, Richardson put at the core of his plays characters entangled in conflicts with members of their community or family. Parents, aunts, cousins, visiting relatives, aging neighbors, grandparents, adopted children, boarders, and lovers fill his stage in plots circling on tensions or rivalries between pairs: brother against brother, boarder against landlord, parent against child, and husband against wife, as he depicted the harm done to the black community by its own members. Without the drama inherent in lynching and the complications of mixed blood, Richardson's plots concern fairly mundane events. Furniture is borrowed against or repossessed, or a woman marries an older man for his relative wealth. Frequently, landlords gossip about the marital status and complexion of boarders. An indigent family in Georgia saves to make the journey north only to have one of its members steal the savings. A real-estate agent bilks a client with an ailing wife out of $500; a thief, struck with paralysis, refuses to ask for God's forgiveness before his death. Such are the problems and situations that the characters face on Richardson's stage.

In his six essays on African-American drama and in several interviews, Richardson commented on the necessity of black drama to have a purpose. To him, much of the value of drama lay in its possibilities for education. The stage was, he held, a teaching space, a platform for education. The African-American playwright had an obligation to instruct the audience on a variety of topics. The audience, more than likely, had moved from the South, leaving behind families and familiar ways of life. In adapting to urban life, they may have found themselves discriminated against in ways that were unfamiliar to them, not only by whites but also by other blacks. Perhaps those in his audiences had to deal with greedy landlords or with suspicious boarders. All in the audience were, more than likely, well aware of the white world that hovered outside of their neighborhoods. African-American plays informed their audiences of social and political conditions affecting them. The plays provided this information indirectly in the form of staged stories. In his 1924 essay, "Propaganda in the Theater," Richardson wrote that although blacks had "worked upon the public opinion with nearly every available method from the prayer meeting to the indignation meeting," the stage, in his opinion, was "one medium which has not been used to any extent" (353). Richardson elaborated on his perception of the stage as being not only able but obliged to "disseminate information" for teaching purposes: "A propaganda play is a play written for the purpose of waging war against certain evils existing among the [black] people in order to gain the sympathy of those people who have seldom, or never, thought upon the subject" (353). He noted that Shaw, Brieux, and Gorki used the stage for "waging war," pointing out that African American playwrights had a similar mission. He did not believe, however, that those changes could come from whites. Instead, he thought that blacks were the chief source of problems that beset the race and should, therefore, address their problems themselves. Believing that "wonders may be done for the cause of the Negro" through propaganda plays written by blacks, Richardson urged that "teaching plays" should "cause those people who are in sympathy with the play's purpose to be up and doing" ("Propaganda" 353). Richardson believed that through his plays he could encourage black people to heed "our duty to strengthen the weak link [the lower-class Negro] rather than to be ashamed of it" ("Characters" 183). Indeed, his comment on the weak link contains the essence of Richardson's intention for his plays: to create via the stage an awareness among African Americans of the necessity for the race to work together.

In urging the use of the stage as an educational medium, Du Bois played an ever-present and crucial role in Richardson's development as a playwright. In his autobiography, Richardson called the black leader his "guide," and, indeed, Du Bois had encouraged Richardson when he began writing for the stage: Richardson's plays in *The Brownies' Book*, his play *The Deacon's Awakening*, and several of his essays on drama had all been published through Du Bois's editorship at *Crisis*. In his role as mentor, spiritual or actual, Du Bois had shaped Richardson's ideas for the stage. Both men believed that through drama, education, whether through plays on black history or in urging mutual support, could most readily and effectively take hold. Because the stage made the abstract visible, concrete, because witnessing a play was a communal event, and because understanding a play did not require literacy, it was the ideal medium to reach many people. In their attempts to educate an audience, both men agreed that the stage should portray aspects of black life relevant to the audience and its values. Following his mentor, Richardson saw the stage as "one of the very best means of getting an idea before the public." Its purpose was neither to pass the time nor to entertain:

When the theatre is placed in a category where it really belongs, and intelligently considered as an educational institution along with the school, we can easily see that there should be some more important reason than [entertainment] for visiting such a place. ("The Negro and the Stage" 310)

Instead, his plays consider the difficulties that arise from issues of age, class, and gender. Blacks who have, for example, succeeded financially, disdain those who haven't fared well. Some of his antagonists, embarrassed by folk ways, abandon or renounce a past rooted in the South, while others turn against the less educated of the race, mocking them for their jobs or living conditions. To Richardson, the weaknesses in the black community often led to the dissolution of the family or neighborhood. We see the damage done in his plays when, for example, black landlords frequently gouge their tenants with high rents, or when black businessmen prey on the gullibility, desperation, and naiveté of the lower classes by luring them into shady deals. Black parents attempt to exert unreasonable control over their grown children or a husband dominates his wife. Lack of support, infidelity, theft, or greed among African Americans are the causes and, at times, the consequences of a tear in the fabric in families and communities. No doubt, Richardson's belief in upholding the community—its necessity for the survival of the black race—goes toward explaining why Richardson, following Du Bois, believed that these plays should be performed in black churches, lodges, schools, and libraries—gathering sites for those who had a common culture. As Richardson pointed out, "*The Chip Woman's Fortune* was about ordinary Black people. In commercial theater ordinary Black plays were not well received. Commercial [white] theater wanted plays about prostitutes, dope handlers, thieves or criminals. . . . They wanted stereotypes" (Willis). Perhaps because Richardson's plots had such mundane characters and plausible events, they portrayed life among African Americans more accurately than did other plays of the decade.

Richardson's plays are further distinguished from those of his contemporaries by the characters he created, especially those of humble means. In his plays, the characters either live in the rural South or are the offspring of parents who have made the trek to the North. His characters have moved from a world where livestock must be fed, where weather controls activities and profits, and where firewood waits to be chopped to one of crime. Accompanying these blacks in their migration to the North's industrial cities were dialect, folk beliefs, and faith in God. The blacks in Richardson's plays are kith and kin to those described by August Wilson in his prefatory remarks to his play *Joe Turner's Come and Gone* (1988):

From the deep South the sons and daughters of newly freed African slaves wander into the city. Isolated, cut off from memory, [f]oreigners in a strange land, they carry as part and parcel of their baggage a long line of separation and dispersement which informs their sensibilities and marks their conduct as they search for ways to reconnect, to reassemble.... ("The Play")

In his urban plays, Richardson portrays these citizens and their progeny, some middle class, some poor, whose lives he examines within the black community as they adapt to urban ways. Now dispersed in, yet disenchanted with, the "Promised Land" of the North, Richardson's characters must find a community in which they feel secure.

Richardson saw "the folk" as having "the soul of a people," writing that "the soul of [African-American] people is truly worth showing" ("Hope" 338). Like white playwright Ridgely Torrence, Richardson realized that the Irish National Theater might serve as a model of what could be achieved if African Americans developed their own theater, one based on their own experiences in America. Both cultures, after all, had been oppressed, and both had a rich folk heritage on which to build a literature. By drawing on African-American folk culture, Richardson believed, a writer could find authentic materials. He supported his belief in this stratum of society by creating powerful and memorable working-class characters: Jane Lee, Aunt Nancy, Emma Turner, Hoggy Wells, Steve Hardy. In fact, his most important plays are his folk plays: *The Flight of the Natives, Compromise, The Broken Banjo, The Hope of the Lowly, The Chip Woman's Fortune, The Deacon's Awakening, Mortgaged, Curse of the Shell-Road Witch, Pillar of the Church*—all contain characters who exemplify his faith in the folk while revealing their weaknesses and occasionally petty ways.

To Richardson, dialect characterized this "distinctly Negro type" (Garvin). In his introduction to *Plays and Pageants from the Life of the Negro* (1930), Richardson wrote that he had purposely omitted plays written in dialect from this collection. Because these plays were intended for school and church productions, he thought that dialect might continue the stereotypes of blacks as uneducated. Nevertheless, he defended its use in his other plays, pointing out that "the dialect of the slave days is still the mother tongue of the American Negro" ("Propaganda" 354).

Richardson's own rural upbringing may explain his affinity to folk culture. As a bricklayer, his father labored manually as did his mother who took in laundry. Several of his folk plays recognize this group and, in some plays, grant working-class African Americans a dignity not ordinarily accorded them either on stage or off. Many (though by no means all) of his folk characters are proud, resourceful, and kind. Rowena Jelliffe of Cleveland's Karamu House read several of Richardson's folk plays and praised his characters for their "dignity [because] that's what [black characters] didn't have back then" (Garvin).

Richardson's lack of both a college degree and social connections seem to have shut him out of the upper stratum of black society in Washington, D.C., which may explain his frequent criticism of successful blacks. Unable to attend college—and obviously capable of and interested in going—Richardson often castigates blacks who have achieved that status. Influenced by either their careers, education, or family ties, these characters frequently abandon less fortunate blacks. The college-educated blacks in his plays tend to be pretentious, smug, and arrogant social climbers.[3] Characters who have gained standing in the community employ chauffeurs, own businesses, hold real estate, play tennis, and, in one play, have children attending Harvard and Smith colleges. However, these same characters ignore or abuse those who are financially or socially weaker.

Richardson could be considered among the first African-American feminist playwrights, for women, his most fully developed characters, hold the most powerful roles in most of his plays. In fact, in nearly all of his plays the women are rarely victims; they frequently control the situation or rescue the family from despair or tragedy.[4] The women in Richardson's plays have a texture and substance rare on the black stage at this time or preceding it. Characters modeled on those in the genteel tradition, such as Grimké's heroine Rachel, are flat characters when compared to Richardson's Jane Lee or Emma Turner. The women in his plays defend their families, stand up for women's rights, care for relatives, financially support husbands who may be involved in unscrupulous activities, and generally keep the family intact. As will be discussed, these female characters play an array of roles: Martha Jones, along with her daughter, is a champion for women's suffrage; Ruth Martin, in contrast to her lazy husband, launders for neighbors and cooks for her family and four boarders; the elderly Aunt Nancy tends to her ailing landlady and gives her landlord her meager savings; Jane Lee attempts to have the man who murdered her husband and son pay for the education of her other children; and Emma Turner uses her savings to help her husband escape. Indeed, it is generally the females in his plays who are the protagonists, the role models for others, and those who come to the aid of the community.

Richardson's female characters are often, however, quite human. In several plays, they complain about the ways and habits of their husbands, or they want money to climb the social ladder, goading their husbands to work harder to keep up the image of success, even if the money is gotten through dishonest methods. They gossip, misjudge, and attempt to play matchmaker. They complain about their maids, their husbands, and their neighbors. They frequently interfere in their children's lives. In considering the plight of the black woman, Richardson's plays frequently look at the various means they use to survive, whatever their situations. The relationships between husbands and wives are often part of Richardson's dramas. Richardson's fiancés and husbands often play minor roles; if they are present, they tend to be ineffectual, lazy, domineering, and blustering. His female characters rarely depend upon men; those who rely on their husbands must cater to their moods or whims because the women are often powerless either to change them or to leave them. Although few of his female characters are submissive, they often go to great lengths to keep peace in the home, realizing that occasionally giving in makes life smoother for all involved.

Because few of his characters are poverty stricken, the possibility of melodrama is further avoided. The plays are thus freed from maudlin episodes and thereby become more realistic. His plays gingerly take the middle course, reflecting black life "as it is" among African Americans (Garvin). The depiction of blacks as suffering "angels" was one of two criticisms directed against the work of black playwrights by several black critics at the time. At the other extreme was the complaint that in plays by whites, African Americans were, as Richardson pointed out, frequently portrayed as "pimps, drug dealers, or thieves." In *The Negro in the Making of America* (1964), Benjamin Quarles identified the very qualities that set Richardson's plays apart from other early African-American plays:

In drama ... the American public was slow to show any interest in the serious portrayal of Negro Life. Budding Negro dramatists like Willis Richardson faced not only white indifference but also the artistic limitations imposed by Negro audiences, who as a rule, did not like dialect, did not like unpleasant endings, and who insisted that all Negro characters be fine, upstanding persons, barely a cut below the angels. (201)

In an interview, Richardson made comments in a similar vein:

Before *The Chip Woman's Fortune*, most of the plays and players were put on stage just to be laughed at, never serious. [They] didn't have a Black man on stage as a serious character. Even the names of plays, Wilson's *Meek Mose* [for example], would show that they weren't too serious. When I started writing I made up my mind that I would be serious about it. (Garvin)

In general, Richardson's characters, rich or poor, are not predictable or cardboard. An audience often sees the same flaws and vices in the lower class as in the upper, with neither group idealized. Along with their good qualities, his African-American characters

can be cruel, jealous, vindictive, greedy, petty, conniving, and dishonest. The primitive or childlike innocent "negro folk" seen in the
plays of Paul Green and Dubose Heyward, both white, and those
characters that are nearly sanctified in works by many of Richardson's African-American contemporaries, are absent.

Believing that the "peasant class of the Negro group has strength
for material in plays," Richardson wrote:

It is not necessary for your leading character to be a criminal, but it is very
necessary for him to be interesting and distinctly a Negro type ... distinctly
different from the white man. The cultured Negro is so much like the cultured white man that he is seldom interestingly different enough to be
typical of the whole Negro race. So to write a play about cultured Negroes
is to very nearly write a play about cultured white people. ("Negro Character" 183)[5]

Prejudice is acknowledged as a fact of life—why deal with it on
stage? he seems to ask. Instead, Richardson's work moves on to
other topics: How does the race confront discrimination among
blacks? How does one deal with African Americans who stand in
the way of the progress of others of the race? How does prejudice
based on the shade of one's complexion hold back the black community? What responsibility do blacks have toward one another?
What are the consequences of the members of the race discriminating against one another? Urging African Americans to take responsibility for their plight, Richardson wraps his tales around "real
black lives." Their commonplace occupations lend his characters
credibility: porters, deacons, real-estate agents, laundresses, boot-
blacks, preachers, sharecroppers, and bootleggers move into his
one-act plays with their problems, chicanery, and anxieties.[6]

In Richardson's plays, the abuse of one character by another
does not necessarily supply the story line. Instead, the lead characters often bring about their own demise or failure through their
own choices or agency. They are frequently their own enemies,
caught in webs of greed, misjudgment, and ambition.

Many of his plays seem to allow an audience to see the damage
blacks inflict on other blacks through their lack of support, especially by those who are successful. According to Richardson, a play
should provide glimpses of life within the African-American com-

munity where such support was not present. Instead of putting his characters in emotional or tragic situations, Richardson placed them in realistic, often mundane, scenarios. Complications arising from miscegenation and passing, for example, are rarely factors in his plays. His play *Compromise* (1926) is one of his very few to depend on a white antagonist.

Richardson's plays are further distinguished from those by other African Americans of the 1920s for their frequent lack of resolution. Dramas by his contemporaries have a conclusion, a traditional and expected denouement; by the final scene, the story has ended and questions have been answered. Usually this resolution comes about through death by lynching or illness. Richardson's plays offer a slice of life; although the curtain may have fallen, the central conflict has not necessarily been settled. An audience member might leave a Richardson play with the sense that the characters still have much to resolve and that their futures may not be favorable. In this non-resolution, or lack of usual closure, the curtain seems to drop *in media res*. The action, it might be said, seems to continue with the unresolved situations only blocked from the audience's view.

In considering his reliance on black characters and situations, on working-class people, and the lack of a comfortable, or predictable, closing, one might divide Richardson's plays into two groups: those drawn from the folk culture, most often in rural Georgia or South Carolina, and those set in a city and centering on the friction between bourgeois and working-class African Americans. His folk characters are the uneducated, the underclass, those who live on the margin of a white world but do not cross that border. His indigent urban dwellers frequently remain linked to their folk past in the South through dialect, the use of roots and herbs, a reliance on the black community, and a faith in God. Those drawn from the middle-class are usually educated, arrogant, self-satisfied, and judgmental. Perhaps this was his judgment of the Talented Tenth, a group that never seemed to accept him. For the most part, this elevated group, once they have succeeded, seems to want little contact with those who are less fortunate. As will be discussed in the next chapter, the characters who have left behind—whether literally or emotionally—their folk past and embraced the city are the very ones who seem to turn their backs on the black community and who fail to respond to its needs, to the detriment of themselves, their families, and, by extension, the black race.

NOTES

1. For a defense of the plays written by 1930 by black women, see the first chapter of Elizabeth Brown-Guillory, *Their Place on the Stage: Black Women Playwrights in America*. New York: Praeger, 1988. Nellie McKay suggests, albeit unwittingly, that there are similarities among many of the plays written by African-American women during the 1920s. See "What Were They Saying?: Black Women Playwrights of the Harlem Renaissance" In Victor A. Kramer, ed. *The Harlem Renaissance Re-examined*. New York: AMS Press, 1987: 129–47. All plays by women discussed here are located in *Black Theater, U.S.A.: Forty-Five Plays by Black Americans: 1847–1974*. James V. Hatch and Ted Shine, eds. (New York: Free Press, 1974.)

2. According to Arthur Davis and Michael Peplow, 3,052 lynchings took place in the United States between 1885 and 1919, which makes obvious the social, indeed the humane, purpose behind anti-lynching plays. See *The New Negro Renaissance*. Arthur P. Davis and Michael Peplow, eds. (New York: Holt, Winston and Rinehart, 1975: 21).

3. Langston Hughes, whom Richardson had met through Carter Woodson, also criticized the upper stratum of African Americans in Washington, D.C. See Langston Hughes, "Our Wonderful Society: Washington" *Opportunity* 5 (1927): 226–27.

4. His reliance on strong female roles may have been influenced by the number of females in his household; with him lived his wife, his three daughters, possibly his mother, and an occasional elderly aunt.

5. Richardson wrote that critic George Jean Nathan, in an essay on African-American dramatists, "spoils the chapter" by labeling blacks as "coons" and as being "porters, waiters and cooks." See George Jean Nathan. "The Black Art." In *Mr. George Jean Nathan Presents* (New York: Knopf, 1917: 115–21).

6. In a 1972 interview, Richardson commented that his play *The Chip Woman's Fortune* was "about ordinary Black people." He recounted going to the Howard Theater to see the effect of the plays on the audience:

One night I was standing in the right wing among the stage hands looking at a performance of *The Chip Woman's Fortune* when I heard one of the stage hands say, "ain't that just like life." I felt at that time and still feel that his simple statement] was one of the finest compliments I have ever received. ("Youth")

4

The African-American Community: The Focus of Willis Richardson's Plays

In his 48 plays, Willis Richardson examined the theme of tensions within the black American community. Through a range of settings and situations, Richardson's plays continually return to this topic. He promoted his belief in black self-help by illustrating the benefits of giving support to others within the black community and the consequences of denying it. For younger readers, *The Children's Treasure*, for example, portrays youngsters who help an elderly, impoverished woman who is to be evicted. By collecting money, the youngsters gather enough resources to prevent her from being put out. *The Black Horseman*, set in Africa in the second century BC, portrays a king who uncovers a traitor to the crown and to the stability of the kingdom. *Rooms for Rent* considers the damage done to a household through the landlady's gossip over the shade of a boarder's complexion.

The offer of help to the community might take any number of forms. Members of a family, boarders, or neighbors give their life savings or provide hiding places for one another. Slaves band together to escape a plantation, or black women encourage other African Americans to vote. In some of his dramas, women advise children and friends, or parents sacrifice to educate their children. The majority of Richardson's plays look at refusals by blacks to help others of the race. The denial of support—emotional, financial, or spiritual—is illustrated in several ways, all of which have consequences more far-reaching than the immediate group or family. In not helping others of the community, a father, out of his need to control the family, prevents his child from attending a particular school. In some plays, parents set poor examples for their children by judging other blacks on the shade of their skin or their lack of financial success. Often a parent prejudges a daughter's fiancé or gossips among friends about a new neighbor or tenant. A father plots with his two daughters to avenge the death of a third daughter by capturing the man who let her drown. A mother encourages her daughter to marry an older man in order to inherit his money. A young man, paralyzed in the act of theft, refuses to ask forgiveness. His mother denies him any sympathy for his plight, commenting that he brought God's wrath on himself.

For the most part, Richardson does not address racial issues in his plays. By not including white characters, Richardson's plots are not delineated by simple black-white/good-bad tensions and the conflicts accompanying those situations. Indeed, the lack of suspense in his plays may explain why his plays, outside of church, civic, and school groups, were not always popular.

Ten plays will be discussed here to illustrate the theme of self-support among African Americans as seen in Richardson's plays. The conflicts are tied to issues of either gender, class, or family. This chapter closes with discussions of three plays in which his African-American characters pool their resources and overcome petty differences to advance the race, even if only in a single household or community.

Although *The Deacon's Awakening* (1920) is known to only a few scholars, the play is significant among early African-American dramas in that it focuses on issues related to gender rather than to race. *The Deacon's Awakening* was published in *Crisis* in November 1920. It was first produced at a union hall in St. Paul, Minnesota, in January 1921. Despite its inauspicious opening in St. Paul—Richardson admitted that the play was "not much of a success" ("Preface" 167)—this play is the earliest African-American feminist drama written by a male, for it addresses the efforts of two men and, by extension, an entire church to undermine the involvement of women in the Voting Society. The play reveals the strategies the women use to encourage voting and to best the men; it reveals also the attempts by the male characters to thwart the efforts of the women.

Set in Washington, D.C. over the course of an afternoon and evening, *The Deacon's Awakening* focuses on Martha and Dave Jones and their 22–year-old daughter, Ruth. Also included in the cast is Eva, Ruth's friend, and Sol, who is both Eva's father and Dave's friend. The play opens with the three women discussing that night's meeting of the Voting Society, an organization that urges black women to vote "now that they have the right." They have been attending meetings covertly; Ruth has, in fact, helped to organize this suffrage group. The deacon's board, however, wants to squelch these activities; to do so, it has appointed Dave Jones to discover the "names of all the women [involved] who belong to our church" so he can "bring the names up before the deacon at the next meeting." Dave tells Sol that the board does not "mean to have women in our congregation goin' to the polls to vote." He believes instead "in a woman stayin' in her place and not tryin' to fill a man's shoes." Learning of his plans to spy on that night's meeting, Martha contrives an excuse for him to visit a sick neighbor instead. On Dave's return, however, Sol relates that Ruth has given a speech at the evening's gathering. When the women arrive, Dave confronts his wife about her involvement in suffrage activities. Presumably for the first time, she stands up to him:

MARTHA: I'm a member of the society and I give money to it—your money. You men think our minds never go further than cooking and darning socks.

DAVE: You can't make me believe in a woman voting.

MARTHA: You'll believe in it of your own accord when you wake up.

By the play's end, Dave Jones has been awakened in two ways: when he learns, much to his chagrin, that his wife and daughter have been urging women to vote, and when his wife asserts herself in defense of women's rights. At the play's close, Martha tells both Dave and Sol, "When we add our strength to yours, you'll get along better. [Women] have been leaving too much to the men." By urging "colored women" to vote, Martha argues for improved conditions, for "It is not a change is coming but," as she points out, "our great trouble is to make you colored men and women aware that [a change] is already here."

Although it is light on the surface, the one-act drama deals with issues on the minds of American men and women at the time—the assertion of a woman's independence through the right to vote and thereby to effect change. In becoming involved with other women through this cause, the women here reveal that they have a life independent of male control. The self-identity his wife and daughter would develop through their activities would, no doubt, weaken or at least change the power Dave Jones now lords over them. The power the women seemed to have gained in speaking out is, however, only superficial; this is evident when one looks beneath the levity and the initial impact of the play. It becomes obvious that sexual stereotypes are very much a part of Richardson's seemingly liberated stage. Even after gaining Dave's reluctant approval about voting, Martha and Ruth Jones are very much subservient to Dave Jones. At the end of the play, as Ruth and Eva prepare dinner for the men, we learn that Martha has been contributing her husband's money to the voting cause. Further, she asks her husband's permission to tell the girls that "It's all right" for them to be involved in the Voting Society. As Richardson's play notes point out, Martha stays ahead of her housework, which might lead one to believe that housekeeping has been her chief activity. Perhaps because Richardson was a male writing about females or because male-female roles were so ingrained and seemingly inflexible at that time, Richardson seems unable to present truly independent women in this first play.

The women in *The Deacon's Awakening* prefigure those in many of Richardson's later plays. Although they may be under the control of the men, they exert what power they can in their circumstances. Those who are married generally must submit to their husbands' demands for order in and control of the home. The women reveal their own opinions and their complaints about their marriages only to other women, who are most often either daughters, neighbors, or boarders.

In a more serious vein and almost as a counterpart to *The Deacon's Awakening*, Richardson wrote *A Pillar of the Church* (192?).[1] This work also examines the control a male exerts over his wife and two daughters. Unlike Dave Martin, John Fisher rules by intimidation.

A fanatically religious man, Fisher instills fear in and tyrannizes his family through religion. It is not the peace of Christ that he preaches, however, but the wrath and control of the Old Testament God. They obey him and keep the home orderly, not through love or respect, but out of fear as he regiments their lives. He insists that the family pray together on their knees each evening. Fisher demands obedience, allowing no one in the home to correct or stand up to him. The purpose of the play, it seems, is simply to illustrate Fisher's control.

Seeing May, his elder daughter, perform a dance for which she has won an award, Fisher is aghast. Her boarding school, he is certain, has ruined her; he forbids the "sinful foolishness" to continue in the house, saying that he will "not allow his house to become a dance hall." Powerless, the women in the household cower, fearful of his anger. In speaking to her mother, May, who has been away at school, questions her father's control over the family: "I really think you let him have his own way too much in everything. He has no consideration for anyone's feelings but his own." Geneva, the younger daughter, is told that, despite a visit from one of the school's teachers, she will not be permitted to attend the school. Her father fears she will be ruined by the novels assigned in English class and the dance exercises in gym. Striking the table with his fist, Fisher tells his wife and younger daughter, "If I can't find a school to suit me, she'll stay right home. That ends it." The play closes with Mrs. Fisher consoling her younger daughter: "When he sets his mind one way he never changes."

That African Americans both male and female were less privileged than whites is irrelevant to Richardson's point in both plays; rather, his point is that men often abuse the power they have in their homes. As the father of three daughters and living with his wife and ailing female relatives, Richardson was more than likely sensitive to the status of females. As African-American men, both John Fisher and Dave Martin may have been frustrated in their jobs and perhaps held subservient positions because they were black. Since this is not mentioned by Richardson, however, it seems that the prejudice they encounter outside the home is either irrelevant or invalid in his promotion of a strong and supportive black family. Unlike *Deacon*, *Pillar* has no victor—neither parent nor child benefits through the religion forced on them, nor the decisions Fisher makes in controlling their lives. As Richardson's stage directions note, Mrs. Fisher's "husband has bullied the soul out of her."

Interestingly, in both plays religion and the church are the guides that the two men follow, yet neither Dave Jones nor John Fisher practices the Christian virtues of mercy, love, and understanding. Instead, they use their spiritual guides—the minister, the church, and Bible—to justify their control over those who are not, at least financially, empowered to break away. In considering these two plays, one might see the church itself as a party to subjugating women, indeed to subjugating the race by not permitting members to question authority. The women are, after all, working to encourage African Americans to vote, not just women. Both Jones and Fisher exemplify Richardson's criticism of organized religion as these men undermine the strength of their families through their zealous control of its members. The men in these plays show the fragmenting of the family when its members are not supporting one another. In these plays, education, voting, and freedom of expression are discouraged, and the household is not the traditional haven or place of refuge; rather, it is a site of silent stress.

The theme of social superiority, of one class looking down on and prejudging another, is the focus of *The Bootblack Lover*. Richardson was awarded the *Crisis* prize for drama in 1927 for this play. Here, the household is upset when Dot Martin, a promising young black woman, falls in love with Hoggy Wells, who polishes shoes and boots to earn a living. Although the Martins are not wealthy—Mrs. Martin is a laundress and Mr. Martin is unemployed—they still have standards that do not include the marriage of their daughter to a bootblack. Nor do the four boarders, who form an extended family, approve of the relationship.

The play opens with the boarders and their landlords, Rachel and Sam Martin, sitting at the dinner table; conversation turns to the bootblack, Wells, and his newly discovered interest in Dot. With Dot in the kitchen, the boarders and the Martins agree that the man is "common," "a bum," and "dirty." Rachel Martin points out that if she has her way, Wells will never "darken that door." Someone mentions that Wells "was a soldier during the big war" and is an honest, although poor, man. All agree that these good points are not enough to redeem him socially and, thereby, make him worthy of Dot's hand.

Contrasted with the humble bootblack is Dot's father, Sam Martin. As in so many of Richardson's plays, the head of the household undermines the goodwill of the family. Although he contributes a minimum amount of time, money, or care to his family's well-being, he still expects to control his small domain. Similar to Dave Jones in *The Deacon's Awakening* and John Fisher in *A Pillar of the Church*, Martin, well fed and argumentative, exerts complete control over the household. In his notes to the play, Richardson describes Martin as a "fat, lazy man . . . who spends most of his time chewing tobacco and sleeping by the fire." Although he hasn't worked in several years, he still commands his wife and daughter from his fireside chair. Overworked, Rachel runs the household, launders clothes for neighbors, and prepares the meals for her family and the four boarders. Although she is disgusted with her husband, she is tied to her responsibilities to her family and to those who rent rooms. As she advises one of the boarders, "When you get married, if you're ever foolish enough to take that crazy step, be sure you marry a man that's willin' to work. . . . That lazy husband of mine, husky as he is, ain't struck a lick of work in four years." Fearing that her daughter will also be ensnared in an unhappy marriage, she pleads that Dot "can do much better than . . . a common bootblack."

Miss Henderson, a boarder, tells Dot that because of the bootblack's low status, she "shouldn't think of paying any attention" to him. Aside from the young woman, all look down on Wells because he is a shoe polisher. Even Wells is keenly aware of the status of his job and how it bears on the judgments others have of him: "What's commoner than kneelin' down in front of people workin' to make their shoes look good while they sit up and read the newspaper or look down on you like you was a dog." He, too, believes that Dot can do much better. Despite the disapproval of her parents and the boarders, and regardless of his self-effacement, Dot continues to profess her love for the bootblack. At a late-night rendezvous, Dot tells the bootblack that she is pregnant by him. In addition to facing her family's admonitions over class differences, she must go to her parents for help. Although he is poor and disapproved of, Wells refuses to abandon her and promises that they will marry. We, however, never learn how her parents received the news of either the pregnancy or the marriage.

The final act is set one year later. Wells has moved in with the Martins and is still a bootblack, and Dot has miscarried the baby. At dinner one evening he announces to all that he is going to expand his business to include the newsstand adjacent to his bootblack operation. He offers Sam, who is still unemployed, the manager's position at the new shop. Surprised and delighted by the prospect of an easy job, Martin, who has objected to Wells all along, accepts the offer. Ruth Martin later points out to her husband how deceptive initial appearances can be: "We all learned a lesson from Hoggy and a good one at that. We know that it ain't the job that makes the man all the time. If it was, you wouldn't be worth a rooster's finger ring." She reminds him of how life has improved for all: "Hoggy's worth somethin' to all of us. Look what he's done for me. Before he came here to live Ah was toilin' in the wash tub six days a week and at night carrying baskets of clothes heavy enough for a mule."

At one time scorned and disapproved of by all but Dot, the bootblack becomes their hero. He not only finds employment for Martin and marries Dot, but he eases Rachel Martin's household chores. The family and boarders notice the improvement in the atmosphere of the home. Everyone is brighter, the home is run more efficiently, and Sam Martin does not seem to complain as often. This might easily be thought of as a simple "rags-to-riches" sort of story, but it is not quite that simple. Richardson does not indicate that the family is wealthy; we can never know whether Sam Martin actually becomes less domineering or whether his job, with Wells as his boss, works out. The playwright reveals no magic formula or *deus ex machina* that saves the day. There is no high drama, no lynching, no lurking white character. Instead, Richardson puts before us a man who has been judged harshly and unfairly. In his simple plot, he reveals that the judgments of the others were inaccurate and nothing more.

The topic of prejudging, of evaluating someone's worth based on initial appearances, recurs throughout Richardson's plays. No matter what the income level, it seems that there is always one group on which another looks down. In fact, Sam Martin, the most judgmental character in *The Bootblack Lover*, is the very one who has the least reason to judge another. Lazy, demanding, sarcastic, and dull, he vigorously opposes Wells. Rather than tending to his household, either financially or with genuine concern, Sam Martin, by his inaction, makes all aware of the drudgery and overwork Dot and Ruth take on to run the household.

The play provides several examples of self-help among its characters. Contrasted with the negativity of Sam Martin are the community and support among those renting rooms in the house, and the compassion they show to Dot and Rachel for the misery of their lives under Martin's control. The boarders seem to have productive lives: they hold jobs, attend meetings, go out together, and discuss the day's activities with one another. The women share recipes and cures, advise Dot, and comfort Rachel. They also admonish Sam for overworking his wife. In fact, it is through a well-intentioned boarder that the Martins hear of Dot's late-night visits with Wells. The women here are especially of interest. Although they are not the focus of the play and are, for the most part, in the background, they are an interesting foil to the Martin family itself. In a sense, the boarders represent how supportive adults interact.

Although other plays by Richardson have groups of women, his female characters do not necessarily form a supportive community. Wives might, for instance, pressure their husbands to earn more money, by whatever means, so they can keep up appearances. In putting the things of this world—material goods and the appearance of wealth—ahead of human compassion, the Cooper family is taught a lesson in *The House of Sham* (1929). Over the course of a day, the family's pretensions are laid open to themselves and to others affected by the manner in which they live and the ends to which they go in order to maintain that life. The main characters are three couples, who provide an interesting contrast to one another: John Cooper and his wife, whose first name is never given; their daughter, Enid, and her fiancé, Dr. Bill Holland, a young doctor; and Joyce Adams, Enid's impoverished cousin, who dates Hal Ford, an employee of John Cooper.

Cooper, as the play reveals, is a hollow man of sorts. He has no money and has, under pressure from his wife and daughter, been upholding a life of appearances. He has complied with the vanity and pretensions of his wife and daughter by supporting their material demands through bank loans and shady deals in his real-estate business. The women, however, are not aware of the degree to which the family is in debt. Pressured to satisfy his wife and daughter materially, John Cooper has built a house of cards. The play focuses on its collapse. By the end, Cooper admits that he has been living beyond his means, although his wife and daughter do not seem to have learned from his experience.

The sham life the Coopers have led crumbles when Dorsey, a former client of John Cooper, seeks the return of the $500 he believes Cooper has cheated him of. With an ill wife and four small children, Dorsey is desperate to have Cooper repay him. Hearing about Dorsey's plight, Cooper shuns any responsibility:

MR. COOPER: Am I supposed to worry my head about that? That's his funeral; he seems to be in a tight place; I can't help it; I didn't put him there.

DORSEY: Ah won't stand by and be kicked around.

When Dorsey threatens Cooper with a revolver, Mrs. Cooper hastily writes out a check for him and Dorsey exits. It is then that the "sham" of the title is made evident. Realizing that the check is "not worth the paper it's written on," Cooper attacks his wife:

MR. COOPER: You've ruined me! ruined me! ruined us all! I haven't got that money in the bank. . . . We don't own a thing. This very house we live in doesn't belong to us. I've been living by my wits, shamming.

He lists her relentless demands for money:

How in the world do you think I ever got money enough to keep you living in your style? Fine clothes, new cars, parties, trips to Europe and everything to try to imitate millionaires. I stole and did everything else crooked and now I'm done for.

Worst of all, perhaps to Mrs. Cooper, is his admission that "We're all done for." He continues: "The whole town will know what I've been doing. Creditors will be on my neck from everywhere." When Joyce, the cousin, calmly suggests that they all go to work, Enid, who is now desperate and angry, replies that Joyce should "think of something reasonable." Still self-assured with her own image in her relationship with her fiancé, Enid smugly offers to let her parents stay with her once she is married to the promising Dr. Holland. She learns, however, that her fiancé, too, has been infected by social pretensions and appearances:

HOLLAND: I'm not quite ready to marry and start a house of my own. I had thought I'd be able to live here with your people until my practice picked up a little.

ENID: I thought your practice was already good.

HOLLAND: No, not anything like it. . . . A fellow has to put up a front, you know. A young doctor has to look prosperous even if he's not. . . . We won't be able to marry for a long time.

ENID: . . . You thought my father was a rich man.

HOLLAND: Everybody thought so.

Holland exits as Enid sobs that she is "sick of all this pretense and sham! Sick to death of it!" Turning to Ford, Joyce tells him she is glad that he doesn't "belong to this house of sham." Although the ending may be trite, the point is clearly that people of value should not live beyond their means, no matter how they wish to appear to others.

At the play's end, Joyce accepts the marriage proposal of Hal Ford, the poor but hard-working, plain man. Perhaps out of jealousy, Mrs. Cooper objects to the marriage. Hal Ford had once been the boyfriend of Enid who had cast him aside in favor of the arrogant young doctor. She argues against a marriage between Joyce and Hal:

MRS. COOPER: You don't make enough money. . . . You couldn't begin to take care of her. . . . [Dr. Holland] has prospects of making plenty of money.

HAL: Dorsey has a sick wife and four hungry children. Whether it's honest or not depends on the way you look at it. They charged more than the owner asked and made a $500 profit.

MRS. COOPER: Everything was lavished on Enid and after she's married she'll expect it . . . what woman can eat and wear good clothes and enjoy herself on the mere fact that her husband is a fine fellow?

The House of Sham argues for both financial and emotional support within a family. Successful blacks should come to the aid of those less fortunate, the "weaker link," or should at least not cheat them. Mr. Cooper's desperation to maintain appearances under pressure from his wife has gone beyond the family; it has hurt the family of Dorsey by bilking him out of $500 in the purchase of his home.

The entire family has been a party to the appearances, the front, they have put up to impress others: John Cooper for the money he has stolen from Dorsey and his implied violence toward the desperate man; Mrs. Cooper for living beyond her means and encouraging Enid to do the same; and Enid herself for basing someone's wealth on appearances, that is, her preference for the foppish Dr. Holland, her pretentious suitor, over the earnest, hard-working Ford.

This play differs from *The Bootblack Lover* in that the ending of *The House of Sham* is bleak. In *The Bootblack Lover*, all of the characters end in a better position, having learned to be less judgmental and to work together. One has a sense that several stumbling blocks have been cleared with the acceptance of the bootblack and the re-employment of Sam Martin. Some characters admit that they erred in judging Hoggy Wells. On the other hand, the Coopers have, by the play's end, suffered for their pretensions and their disdain for those less fortunate; still, we are never assured that they will change their ways.

The tension in the mother-daughter relationship of Mrs. Cooper and Enid is even more heightened when compared to that of similar relationships in *The Deacon's Awakening*, *A Pillar of the Church*, and *The Bootblack Lover*. Indeed, nearly all the relationships among women in Richardson's plays are strong and healthy except for this one. Richardson frequently portrays a mother as the model and guide to the daughter or at least as the daughter's sounding board and support in times of distress. *The House of Sham* follows the same pattern of the mother serving as model. In this play, however, Mrs. Cooper is a negative model in that both Cooper women are ensnared by the appearance of having wealth; Enid has indeed followed in her mother's footsteps. Joyce, as a visiting relative, is not involved in their greed, but she serves as a foil to their machinations and pretense.

A similar mother-daughter relationship is explored in *The Man Who Married a Young Wife*. The theme of aspiring to wealth, no matter how gained, is probed once again. In this play, however, unlike *The House of Sham*, the Barber family is poverty-stricken. Dave and Mamie, the parents, plot with their daughter Ida to marry a neighbor who is believed to be wealthy. Nearly 60 years of age, Dan Simmons seems respectable enough, but more importantly, he is believed to have large sums of money hidden in his house. Through this marriage for money, at least, Ida will be able to live comfortably. She may even be able to contribute some money to her parents. Dan is thrilled at the prospect of marriage to Ida, a woman of 20. He promises her furs, clothing, and a house—things she has barely dared to dream would ever be hers. Ida forsakes Joe Harley, her steady boyfriend, and, with her mother's wishes, snares Dan Simmons.

Two weeks after the wedding, however, Ida is unhappy and complains about Dan's stinginess. He has not given her the things he promised in their brief courtship. Seeking his supposed fortune, she and her former lover, Joe, go though his desk. Dan returns to find Ida and Joe counting the mix of legal and confederate bills, worth only $45. The play ends unresolved with Ida and Joe, both angry, leaving together and Dan saying that he's been used.

Richardson's female characters provide an interesting contrast to those found in the plays of Georgia Johnson and other female playwrights of the decade. His females seem to be either conniving and controlling or the organizing and benevolent force in the families he portrays. To say that Richardson's plays are misogynistic would be too facile. The female characters he creates who are poor frequently seem too desperate and driven to survive by whatever means, rather than cruel.

His play *Rooms for Rent* offers another type of female character, Ma Roberson. Because the family needs the income earned from renting out rooms, she must give up her room and sleep on the sofa. Disgruntled by her loss of space and privacy, she takes out her anger by criticizing the light complexion of the new roomer's baby. To her, the infant looks "mighty white." Frustrated because the family refuses to evict the young mother, Ma complains that she has given enough to the household: "Ah think Ah already helped yer out enough der way ah sweated over der wash tub ter keep a piece o' bread in yo' mouth and a rag on yo' back while yer was gittin' a little ejucation." Her family finally listens to her complaints when she points out that the new roomer, in addition to having a seemingly white child, does not wear a wedding band. Ma intends to have Jennie admit that the child was born out of wedlock. It is not this possibility, however, that upsets the older women; instead, it is that the father is believed to be a white man. For this reason, the Robersons question her, watch her, and plan to shun her. Ma asks her where her husband is, what he does for a living, and if he is going to visit her soon. She fears that the neighbors will talk. It turns out that the boarder's husband "belongs to the upper class. . . . His people have money and didn't want us to marry."

During the discussion, Thornton Wicks, Jennie's husband, arrives. Having located a job in another city, he is now able to have his family join him. After realizing that their suspicions were unfounded, the family asks her to stay on. She refuses "after what's been said." The couple leaves to pack for the next day's trip, with the Robersons left poorer by the lost income and for their hasty and biased judgment.

The pettiness of the Roberson family and their suspicions of the young woman are the focus of this play; that the family is poor is irrelevant. Richardson does not necessarily point his finger at the upper class in his plays; rather, it is at the entire black community. He is no doubt warning against making judgments based solely on appearances. He is also, however, providing a glimpse into the lives of urban blacks and their means of making ends meet.

In *Mortgaged*, Richardson focuses once again on money and the lack of it, this time within a family. Although several of Richardson's plays deal with the power men have over women in the household, *Mortgaged* is about class distinctions. As he does in *The House of Sham*, Richardson probes the pretensions of the upper class, frequently suggesting that their money was made by dishonest means. Perhaps they have forsaken those less fortunate by charging high rents on substandard housing or maybe they have cheated them out of money or have shunned the "weaker link." Yet, as Richardson pointed out, it is this weaker link that African Americans should help to strengthen.

Nearly all of Richardson's plays focus on the black family. Its strength is determined, according to his plays, by the support its members give to one another. *Mortgaged* (1924), in which one brother turns against another, centers again on the pretensions of those who attempt to appear wealthier than they are.[2] John Fields, a widower, struggles financially as he attempts to raise a college-age son alone. A dedicated chemist, he tries to balance his commitment to his laboratory work while he looks for means to pay for his son's upcoming tuition at Harvard University. Tom Fields, the brother of the protagonist, and Tom's wife, Mary, have spun their lives, it seems, around keeping up with their neighbors. Through Tom Fields's lucrative rental properties, they have been able to maintain their social standing. The couple is, thus, embarrassed by John Fields's lack of status and money.

As the play opens, the children of Tom and Mary prepare to leave to play tennis as they discuss the coming semesters at Smith College and Harvard University. Financially secure, the Fields agree to loan his brother, John, the money for his son's tuition with a stipulation: John Fields must abandon his laboratory research and seek regular employment with a steady income.

The plot is marred by the contrivance of having money arrive just in time. As John Fields is about to agree to give up his research, the one goal to which he is committed, he learns that a major chemical company has bought one of his formulas. In receiving an advance for it, he is spared from further humiliation at the hands of his brother. With his dignity and independence restored, John is able to tell his brother how little he respects him. A slumlord, Tom Fields has made substantial sums by extracting high rents from his impoverished tenants:

THOMAS: The high rents [the tenants] pay is their penalty for being poor.

JOHN: It's true the poor always have to pay, but in my opinion, the rich owe them something too.

The play ends with the prospect of receiving money from a chemical company for John as he castigates his brother for his superficial values.

Unlike Richardson's other plays, the characters in Mortgaged refer specifically to the status of African Americans. When the sons of two brothers find that they will be attending the same college, they agree to spend time together because "a colored freshman's life must be like a graveyard." In proposing that John Fields get a job "out West" as a chemist, Mary Fields remarks that because of his experience and ability "any firm will be willing to overlook his color." Furthermore, after Tom Fields agrees to loan his brother his son's college tuition on certain conditions, John lashes out:

Perhaps you think you're helping to advance the race by piling up dollars, but you're not! It's not money that's going to make this race of ours respected, but what its men and women accomplish in science and the arts—things that you and your kind know nothing about. . . . If nothing is ever done to make the race respected, you'll soon find out that your dollar that you love so well is not worth as much as the other fellow's dollar!

Mortgaged criticizes not only the successful members of black society for discriminating against another but also family members who do not help one another. Mrs. Fields urges her husband to "be rid of" his chemist brother because "he doesn't amount to anything socially" and "he will never amount to anything financially." The ending of the play suggests that Tom and Mary Fields will not change their ways, for they don't want their children to know of the conditions they made in offering John Fields, their uncle, the loan.

Richardson explores family loyalty and support once again in *The Broken Banjo* (1925) as he examines the outcome of long-standing dissension and mistrust within a family.[3] The tension is brought to an end when two cousins arrange to have Matt Turner, who is related to them by marriage, arrested for a murder he committed several years earlier. An impoverished young married couple, Matt and his wife, Emma, frequently argue over Matt's playing of his banjo. Emma complains that instead of splitting wood and helping her, he spends his time playing the instrument. It seems to her that he doesn't "care a thing about nobody or nothin' but that old banjo." Although he admits he is not talented, he points out that "his banjo is his religion." During an argument over the instrument, the subject of her brother Sam and cousin Adam comes up. Calling them "loafin' jailbirds," Matt dislikes their visits because they "eat eve'ything they c'n get." He also feels slighted by the attention she gives to the malingerers.

Doubting his wife's love for him, he complains that no one likes him except his wife and she "ain't crazy about" him. Emma corrects him: "Ah'm thinkin' for you eve'y minute o' ma life, but you don't know it. You never will know it till you get in a big pinch." Her love for him is proven by a later incident at the close of the play. When Adam and Sam stop by, Matt does not want them to come in, and they refuse to leave the house. Emma attempts to defuse the tension by having Matt run an errand. While he is gone, the two men, playing with his treasured banjo, break it. Fearing Matt's anger, Emma hides the damaged instrument in the closet. On his return, Matt finds the broken banjo, and a scuffle ensues.

When Matt threatens to throw a chair at Sam, Sam blurts out that he knows that Matt was the person who had, several years earlier, killed "old man Shelton." Realizing that he is in their power, Matt, after locking the men in the room with him, forces them to swear on the Bible that they won't divulge his crime. Although the men vow to keep the secret, Matt knows that "as soon as Sam gets full of moonshine whiskey, he'll tell everything he knows." Emma too realizes that discovery and arrest of her husband is imminent once the two men leave. She withdraws 140 dollars she stitched into the mattress and packs a bundle of clothing and bread for his escape. Relying on the family for protection, she tells her husband, "You go out the back way cross the field to Uncle Silas' and get him to row you cross the river to A'nt Linda's and tell huh to hide you till Ah come." As he is about to escape, however, Sam arrives with a white sheriff, who handcuffs Matt and leads him away as Emma is left behind crying.

It is difficult not to have mixed thoughts about the ending of this short play. After all, Matt Turner has committed a murder and has, until now, gotten away with it. Nevertheless, the betrayal of his kin through marriage was unnecessary in that it was done only out of malice. One might ask about the concern Sam and Adam have for Emma, who has fed them and taken them in—indeed, even defended them—to her husband's dismay. Her future seems to be of no concern to the two men who turn in Matt to get even with him for threatening them.

Similar to *The Chip Woman's Fortune* and *The Bootblack Lover*, the figure who seems to offer the least, the weak link, is the very one who comes forward to hold the family together. As with so many of Richardson's other female characters, Emma Turner is the strength of the story. She is the one who has worked the hardest, who has put aside money, who, in a Christian manner, has cared for those rejected by her husband, and who seems to have the family ties across the river who will hide Matt from the sheriff. Yet she is the one who is most damaged by the actions of all the men involved, men who are supposedly close to her—her husband, brother and cousin. As the curtain falls, Emma is left alone, in tears. We do not know what will become of those involved.

Richardson's stage world was not always so grim. Two of his plays in particular feature people who benefit because all involved have offered mutual support, no matter how humble. Both plays portray southern blacks who live in the direst conditions: one group is enslaved, the other lives at the poverty level. The play most frequently mentioned in discussions of Richardson's work, *The Chip Woman's Fortune*, focuses on the theme of cooperation. According to Richardson's plays, membership in a church does not guarantee a loving household. The pride and faith of Dave Jones and John Fisher distance these men from healthy relationships with their families. Unlike the Fieldses and the Coopers, the characters in *The Chip Woman's Fortune* are not interested in impressing others, only in raising their families, living peacefully, and eking out a simple existence. Rather than looking to the head of the household for strength, Richardson's characters in *The Chip Woman's Fortune* turn to the least likely source of aid. As with Emma Turner and Hoggy Wells, the most financially distressed character is of most help to the family. The chip woman, believed to have little of value, is able to aid the Greens, through the savings she has buried.

The play is, as Richardson remarked in 1972, "about ordinary black people" (Garvin).[4] In the space of one afternoon, the financial predicament of the Green family is solved through the aid of Aunt Nancy, an elderly, poverty-stricken boarder. Known as the chip woman for the pieces of coal and wood she gathers, Aunt Nancy sells what she can and contributes the rest to the household in exchange for a place to sleep. Although it is a meager amount, the money Aunt Nancy has scraped together, her "fortune," is being saved for her son Jim, who is soon to be released from the penitentiary.

The central predicament is over the repossession of the family's new Victrola, their "one source of joy." Because he has fallen behind on the installments for it, Silas Green, Aunt Nancy's landlord, is "furloughed" from his job as a store porter. When the men from the store arrive to repossess it, Silas stalls them. As they wait, Nancy's son Jim arrives. Hearing of the family's plight, he asks his mother to give the Greens the money she has saved for him. Aunt Nancy pays off the Greens' debt. As Silas prepares to return to work, Aunt Nancy promises to supply Liza with more of the root mixture that has relieved her ailments and to return to help her. Refusing to make any arrangements for repayment, Aunt Nancy leaves with Jim.

We never have any clues about what the future holds for either the Greens or Aunt Nancy and her son. After the chip woman leaves, the family still has financial problems to contend with, made even more grave without her contribution of chips of wood and coal. Despite these untied threads and the simplicity of the plot, the play has merit in that it illustrates once again the necessity of blacks depending on one another. The problems have been brought on the Greens through their own choices—the purchase of the Victrola and the lack of payments for it—and they have been re-solved through the aid of another black. With its focus on simple human charity, *The Chip Woman's Fortune* can be read as a morality play. Aunt Nancy, the protagonist, is presented as a nearly Christlike figure. Thought by the Greens to be poor and helpless, she prevents the repossession of their single prized possession.

The play also has merit if one considers its intended audience. More than likely, those who saw the play were relatively new to a city and to the opportunity to purchase household items on time. Perhaps to make ends meet, those who saw the play rented rooms to boarders. Several of Richardson's plays include tenants and landlords and their relationships. The whites here, principally the store owner for whom Green works, are not cast as villains; rather, the store owner simply wants his due payment for the item.

The small group works out its own problems. Although she pays no rent, Aunt Nancy has helped the family in several ways. With the roots she gathers in the woods, she concocts a cure for Liza Green's illness. Aunt Nancy also gathers chips of wood and coal for the family's heat. When Liza is despondent over the family's fi-nances and her own illness, Aunt Nancy boosts her spirits. She also urges Liza not to be overly critical of Emma, the Greens' teenage daughter. The Greens have taken in Aunt Nancy and received no cash for that, only the contribution of fuel for heating and cooking. Among the most benevolent of Richardson's characters, Aunt Nancy is, however, not to be completely sanctified. Her character is made credible by her initial ignoring of the family's financial plight. Although she is aware of the Greens' need for money, she doesn't offer to help them until her son prods her to do so.

Another example of self-help within a group is shown in *Flight of the Natives* (1927). First published in Locke's *Plays of Negro Life* (1927), *The Flight of the Natives* was initially written as a one-act play. First produced by the Krigwa Players in Washington, D.C., on 7 May 1927, the play became a popular choice with theater groups at black schools. In 1964, Richardson expanded it to three acts. Once again, the focus is the strength derived from the unity of a group with a common aim, which in this case is their escape from Marsa John, the plantation owner. In order to be successful, the escape must be a joint effort, and each person is assigned his or her own role. Called a "historical drama" by Bernard Peterson, the play includes comic and dramatic elements. Its variety of characters, all with individual personalities, however, is too much for an audience to absorb in a single act. The varieties of action—a beating, two escapes, an argument, disguises—are complicated by the variety of responses evoked from the audience—joy, fear, pity, and anger. The range of emotions and actions may explain why the playwright, during the 1960s, revised the play into three acts. In the revision, Richardson added the character of black female abolitionist Sojourner Truth. Set in the rural South, it is one of Richardson's few plays to include white characters.

One of his more complex plays, *Flight* has two points of conflict: the white master who threatens to sell the slave husbands so their wives will never see them again, and the treachery of the slave Jude, who connives to turn in any slaves plotting to escape. *Flight* sets up one slave as antagonistic to the other slaves, who plot to escape. The range of characters adds to the quality of the play, making it perhaps Richardson's best work: strong women who stand by their husbands, proud black men; it is Luke, however, the slave considered "ondependable [sic]" by the others, who devises the escape plan.

The play opens with news of the recapture of Slim, an escaped slave. The other slaves fear their own safety, for Mose, a slave, knew of Slim's planned escape and did not report it. He threatens to strike the slave Jude, who betrayed Slim's escape to "Marsa John." Because of his threats, Mose is told he will be sold "down the river in the morning," away from Pet, his wife. The six slaves—two married couples and two other men—decide that they must devise some way to "breathe the air deep, and know [they] ain't no mo' slave." Luke, considered the most shiftless of the group, states that "The Lawd help us all, fo' we need deliv'rance." He tells the others that he has a plan and they are not to question what he asks of them. Monk, who whips the slaves, and Jude are to be tricked and locked in the woodshed. Slim will be set free to join the others. With two of the men hidden, Sally tells Master John that they have escaped by boat. Believing her, he sets out in search of them. Luke devises a plan whereby all can escape. He appears at the cabin door dressed in a planter's costume and directs the slaves to follow him off of the plantation. He is going to pass as the slave owner: "Now, folks, 'me-mbah! You-alls my niggahs when we get away from heah. . . . you-all's jes' been purchus,' understand that? An' we-all had to turn off de road after Slim, 'cause he run away—and yo' helpin' me back with him." The play closes as Luke with a "commanding gesture marshals them out the door and closes it." Through masking and by pooling their resources, the slaves make their escape. To effect it, they use the difference in skin shade to their advantage. As Richardson's stage notes point out, Luke is "evidently a mulatto, and illegitimate son." Having the lightest complexion, he poses as and is able to pass for a white slave-owner who is taking his recaptured slaves home. By joining forces, the slaves escape, although the audience never learns if they are successful.

First produced by Karamu House in Cleveland, *Compromise* is one of the few plays Richardson wrote that has a white antagonist. Set in "a country district of Maryland," the play is perhaps Richardson's most complex.

The plot focuses on the problems the Lee family has endured because of Ben Carter, a wealthy, white neighbor. Seven years earlier Carter accidentally shot and killed Jane Lee's oldest son, Joe, for stealing apples. Carter attempts to quiet the family by paying off Joe's father with $100, which the father uses to get drunk. Lee too drinks, and his drinking is fatal. Learning of his sister's pregnancy by Carter's son, Alec hits him and breaks his arm. Ben Carter comes to the Lee house seeking revenge as Alec prepares to escape to a relative's house. The play ends with Jane Lee loading the shotgun to take revenge on the Carter family for the deaths and trouble they have brought to her family.

Jane Lee is perhaps the strongest female character among Richardson's plays. Like Aunt Nancy in *The Chip Woman's Fortune*, Jane

Lee is strong and good-hearted and has suffered because of her family. After learning of Annie's pregnancy, Jane Lee strikes a compromise with Carter that in return for the trouble his family has caused hers, he will pay for the education of her other daughter, Ruth, and her son Alec. She has suffered two deaths and poverty, and she has raised three children alone. Several times she remarks on the injustices that follow blacks because of their skin color. At one point, she remarks to Ben Carter that if she and her family had been white, he would not have been able to cover up, or "compromise" with $100, the death of their son Joe as he did.

NOTES

1. *Lost Plays of the Harlem Renaissance* includes the first publication of *A Pillar of the Church*. Neither Hatch nor this writer knows the year in which the play was written. Leo Hamalian and James V. Hatch, eds. *The Lost Plays of the Harlem Renaissance, 1920–1940.* Detroit: Wayne State UP, 1996.

2. *Mortgaged* was popular among drama groups at black schools that were seeking plays written by African Americans. In 1925, the play won fourth place in a drama tournament in Plainfield, N.J. About the competition, Richardson wrote:

The rare thing about this occasion was that out of the eight or ten [drama] clubs producing plays, one Negro club produced a Negro play by a Negro author. [*Mortgaged* competed with] some of the best American one-acters. (Introduction to *The Broken Banjo* 167)

3. The play seems to be the one to which Richardson was personally most attached, for he mentioned it in several of his notes. In 1965, he revised it into two different three-act versions, both of which are located at the Schomburg Center for Research in Black Culture. Richardson spent more time revising this play over the years than any of his other works. In interviews and letters, he recounted the following story:

At the beginning of the Harlem Renaissance I sent my play *The Broken Banjo* to the *Crisis* contest for the Spingarn Prize, and in August of that year, Dr. Du Bois sent me a telegram informing me that I had won the first prize and inviting me to come to New York for the presentation ceremonies. ("The Play Prizes")

In April 1928, *The Broken Banjo* was presented by the Dixwell Players and awarded the Edith Fisher Schwab Cup by Yale University. This prize was awarded annually in a nonprofessional drama tournament, which was sponsored by the Drama Committee of the Board of Education in New

Haven; the purpose of the competition was to "rais[e] the standards of both directing and acting." Schwab took "especial interest and pleasure in dramatics in New Haven" (Play Program). Richardson's most widely anthologized play, *The Broken Banjo*, won first place in the *Crisis* Drama Awards in 1925 and was published there in two installments the following year.

4. Published in *Crisis* in 1922, after playing briefly on Broadway, *The Chip Woman's Fortune* opened in Chicago on 23 January 1923 and in Harlem at the Lafayette Theatre on 7 May 1923.

5

An Overview of Other Materials by Willis Richardson

In addition to his folk plays, Willis Richardson's most important contribution to the development of African-American drama are his plays on black history. Through these, he again reveals his belief in the black community and in the stage as a place of education. His interest in writing and compiling plays on black history seems to have come about through his association with Carter G. Woodson. Frequently overlooked in discussions of African-American literature, Woodson was among its greatest champions. The son of former slaves, Woodson, after earning a Ph.D. from Harvard University in 1912, committed his life to the recovery of black history from a black perspective. One of the founding members of the Association for the Study of Negro Life and History in 1915, he had, by 1930, researched and written on African Americans in relation to Reconstruction, urbanization, religion, and slavery. Like Richardson, Woodson "moved away from interpreting blacks solely as victims of white oppressors" (Goggin 67). Richardson's plays, with their absence of white antagonists and his belief in using drama as a means of reaching people to educate them, dovetailed with Woodson's plans and philosophy of recovering and teaching black history.

Richardson wrote in his autobiography that the two men met at Georgia Johnson's salon gatherings in the late 1920s, more than

likely in 1927. Woodson asked Richardson to gather and edit a series of plays that could be used in black schools and colleges for the
purpose of teaching black history. Woodson had apparently approached Du Bois about the same project, for Du Bois mentioned it
in a letter to Locke.

Jean Hall, one of Richardson's daughters, recalled that, aside
from *Crisis* and *Opportunity* magazines, Richardson "could never
get anyone to publish his plays [outside of magazines] until he met
Carter G. Woodson." Editor of the *Journal of Negro History*, which he
had helped establish in 1915, Woodson was the founder of Negro
History Week in 1925. In *Dusk of Dawn* (1940), Du Bois wrote that
the creation of Negro History Week was "the greatest single accom-
plishment to arise from the artistic movement of blacks during the
1920s" (qtd. in Goggin 84). Woodson also headed Associated Publishers, an African-American press located in Washington, D.C. His
interest in improving black education and raising the awareness
among African Americans about their history led to his interest in
the stage as a means of reaching black people, both traditional students and adults. Seeking appropriate materials for class productions, black teachers throughout the South had repeatedly written
to Woodson, asking him whether he knew of any collections of
plays by African Americans. Richardson first met Woodson when
the latter taught history at the M Street School, and their acquain-
tance was renewed at a meeting of the Saturday Nighters: "[Carter]
Woodson came a couple of times," according to Richardson, "when
he wanted me to edit the first book, and when he wanted me to edit
the second book he came" (Garvin).

According to an unpublished letter from Du Bois to Locke, dated
14 May 1927, Woodson had first approached Du Bois about creating the volume that would become *Plays and Pageants from the Life of
the Negro*. As Du Bois wrote,

I did not have a chance to tell you last Sunday when I saw you that Woodson a year ago had asked me to edit a book of Negro plays to be used for
schools. . . . I have not had a chance to do much toward it, and maybe he
will have changed his mind by the time I get to it. I thought, however, I
ought to mention this to you. (Letter to Locke)

Du Bois may have suggested to Woodson that he contact Richardson about the anthology. Through Woodson's Associated Publish-

ers, the playwright edited two collections of plays. The first, *Plays and Pageants from the Life of the Negro* (1930), included Richardson's introduction and four of his plays. The second collection appeared five years later when Woodson again contacted Richardson: "[Woodson] said the first book had gone so well, he asked me if I would edit another one. He asked me if I was superstitious.... I was to collect thirteen plays from different people" (Garvin). The result was *Negro History in Thirteen Plays* (1935), the first and only collection of plays on black history. Although Richardson edited the collection, May Miller's name, at her father's insistence, appears with his on the title page.[1] Scholars, however, continue to credit her as the volume's coeditor.

The interest in "things black," that is, in a life apart from white culture, began to develop more obviously in the 1920s. For perhaps the first time, Americans of African descent, a population that had been denied the benefits that whites enjoyed, considered the ramifications of freedom and the nearly spiritual necessity of locating and identifying a voice that was its own. Primed during the second decade of the twentieth century by Du Bois's pan–African movement and Garvey's call for a return to Africa, African Americans more than ever questioned their origins and history. Africa: What did it mean to an African American? What *was* black history? Was there even a black history, one worth recovering, before the Middle Passage? And where would this be found? How would one learn about black heroes? What was the black story of America? Where was the literature by African Americans? For African–American writers, however, these queries could be subsumed under one overarching question: As African Americans, who are we?

In 1919, Carter G. Woodson, as a black publisher, historian, and essayist, voiced concern about the lack of accurate depictions on the stage or in print:

There is little effort to set forth what the race has thought and felt and done as a contribution to the world's accumulation of knowledge and the welfare of mankind. ... The general reader does not have much insight as to what the Negro was, how the Negro developed from period to period, and reaction of the race to what was going on around it. (275)[2]

In his review of the collection for *The Journal of Negro History*, Woodson wrote, "The plays, being intended primarily for the stage, are adapted in the main to the capacity of children in the various grades of elementary and high schools. Only three or four will meet the requirements of advanced students in college or those on the stage" (Review of *Plays and Pageants*, 263).

The collection had two purposes: to substitute the stereotypes of blacks on stage with positive images; and to address the problem of school curricula, which "as a general thing, [carried] no courses bearing on Negro life and history" ("Negro Life" 277). In his book *The Miseducation of the Negro*, Woodson pointed out that "Negro students [in English courses] should not spend all their time . . . in advanced work on Shakespeare, Chaucer and Anglo–Saxon [*sic*]." Black students should instead, Woodson believed, "direct their attention . . . to the works of Negro writers" (150). "What this age needs," he wrote, "is an enlightened youth . . . to imbibe the spirit of great [African] men and answer the present call of duty with equal nobleness of soul" (138). He urged that books of African-American literature be compiled so that "Negroes should read some things written by their own people that they may be inspired thereby" ("Some Things" 34–35).

Part of Woodson's legacy to black studies, *Plays and Pageants* was intended to remedy this situation, at least partially, on the grade school, high school, and college levels in black schools. The purpose of the collection was to make available to African-American students the heroes and achievers of as well as incidents from African-American history and heritage. The book gave teachers a collection of materials to use in teaching black students their own history. Woodson hoped to engage them in actively learning that history by having them participate in stage works written by African Americans.

Richardson contributed to and edited another anthology of plays: *Negro History in Thirteen Plays* (1935), with May Miller. To this collection, Richardson contributed *Antonio Maceo; Attucks, The Martyr,* also entitled *Crispus Attucks and A Killing in Boston; The Elder Dumas; Near Calvary;* and *In Menelik's Court.* As he noted in the book's half–page preface, "The writers have not attempted to reproduce definitive history, but have sought to create the atmosphere of a time past or the portrait of a memorable figure" (vi). In his review of the book, which his Associated Publishers had produced, Woodson commented that the collection would "find a place in all institutions of learning where an effort is being made to teach the Negro of his own background.... The Americanized or Europeanized Negro is much more highly entertained by the dramatization of distinguished Europeans in the roles of harlots and murderers than by that of Africans as patriots and heroes" (Review of *Negro History* 75) Woodson held that the "proper presentation" of blacks would come from "poets and dramatists who use[d] their art to introduce the world to a new scene of Black life" (*Review* 75–76).

In addition to the plays for *Negro History*, Richardson wrote several others on black history: *Caspard the Oppressor* (192?), *The Black Horseman* (1935), *Invitation to a Duel* (193?), and *Fight for Freedom* (193?).

Richardson is the first African–American playwright to have developed a body of plays explicitly for black children. Simple, one-act morality tales, their themes are brotherhood and understanding among the races; many of his plays promote racial pride among black children. Published in *The Brownies' Book* were *The King's Dilemma* (December 1920); *The Gypsy's Finger-Ring* (March 1921); *The Children's Treasure* (June 1921); and *The Dragon's Tooth* (October 1921). In 1956, Associated Publishers issued Richardson's collection of plays for children, *The King's Dilemma*. The volume included his earlier plays from *The Brownies' Book* as well as new plays. These simple plays have themes that urge equality and kindness to others. In the title play, *The King's Dilemma*, a white child refuses to follow the wishes of his father, the king, who wants him to give up his friendship with a black child. In *The Gypsy's Finger-Ring*, three children meet a gypsy who allows each child to wear her magical ring. By wearing it, each child can choose to see into either the past, the present, or the future. The picture of the past is of black slavery, and the present reveals the situation of the Jews in London at the time. The future, however, is revealed as a time when "the whole five races [are] in harmony, all working side by side for the good of all" (*The Gypsy's Finger-Ring* 71). *The Children's Treasure* centers on the arrival of the "rent man" and his eviction of a penniless, elderly woman. Five neighborhood children combine their pennies to prevent her from moving to the poor house. *The Dragon's Tooth* takes place in "the ancient world when the coming of Christ and the fall of the Roman Empire were dreams of the distant future." A soothsayer tells four children of a dragon's skeleton that has carved on its tooth the secret of the world's future happiness. After they recover the tooth, the soothsayer reveals its cryptic message to them: "The secret of the future good of the world depends upon the growth of Love and Brotherhood. Liberty, Equality, and Fraternity must rule the world in the place of Inequality, Envy and Hate."

Despite attempts later in his life, most of what Willis Richardson wrote has remained unpublished. Several of his play scripts are still bound in the brown wrapping paper he wrapped them in. Some are carbon copies held together by paper clips. In 1994, several manuscripts were found on a shelf in Rowena Jelliffe's hall closet after her death. Richardson's uncompleted cycle of short stories is also in manuscript form. In its original one-act version, Richardson's play *The Broken Banjo* was published in several anthologies and produced by several blacks schools. In the 1960s Richardson lengthened it to three acts. Apparently dissatisfied with it, he again revised it. Both versions of the play are now located at the Schomburg Center for Research in Black Culture, New York Public Library.

Like those discussed earlier, Richardson's other plays are set within the black community and are often set within a home. *Victims* (originally titled *The Deep Regret*) (192?) centers on a mother and daughter who desperately need $50. In order to borrow the money, they put up their living room furniture as collateral. They believe that Mr. Anderson, who works as a porter at an expensive hotel during the winter in Florida, will return home having earned a substantial amount of money. When he returns, however, he reports that he didn't make anything; the family's furniture is repossessed. In *The Idle Head* (1929), a young man, in an effort to help his struggling mother, steals an expensive pin left on a piece of clothing to be laundered by his mother. The plot of *Imp of the Devil* (192?) revolves around the paralysis of a young man who is unrepentant for the life he has led. Because his family lacks the money for a cure, he eventually dies. At the end, Ma Dorsey, his mother, says that his prayers for a cure from God "didn't come from his heart, they only come [*sic*] from his lips, the imp." *Family Discord* (192?), a three-act comedy reveals the problems that beset a family when Dave visits his family with his new bride. By all appearances she is white. As one character says, "I've studied her for fifteen minutes and there's nothing colored about her." Rather than focusing on race issues, however, the play examines the family's struggle to accept Dave's marriage.

Mrs. Mason, in *The Peacock's Feather* (192?), hires herself out as a maid in a wealthy home in order to earn money for her teenage son. Invited as a guest to a party there, her son does not acknowledge that the woman serving him is his mother. The pretensions of the matronly employer, of Mrs. Mason, and of their respective teenagers are disclosed at the play's end. In *The Bold Lover* (192?), two young men discover that they are engaged to the same woman. At a party, the engagement of Joyzelle Farley to George Cookson is to be announced by Mrs. Farley, a society matron. Joyzelle, however, confides to her friend that she loves Gilbert Stewart. Upset by this news, Mrs. Farley decides that the engagement will be announced regardless. The two men meet to discuss upcoming marriages, not realizing that both are engaged to Joyzelle.

Although the title *The Nude Siren* (1929?) is actually the name of a book one of the characters is reading, it created problems for Richardson and the Krigwa Players. In February, 1929, *Crisis* reported that the play was banned for being "too suggestive of immorality":

This is the first time a play of Negro origin has been banned in this way. The Krigwa Players have never had a place to produce their plays outside of the public school buildings, and so this action on the part of the authorities halts their productions for the time being. ("Washington and Virginia" 89)

Several of Richardson's plays deal with magic or spirituality. *The Curse of the Shell-Road Witch* (192?) is believed to have been based on the short story "The Shell Road Witch," which was published in *Crisis* in 1914. In the play, Aunt Dinah, an elderly woman in a Florida community, casts a spell on Mandy Smith, her neighbor, when Smith refuses to give her food she has prepared for the preacher's visit. Learning of the spell, the minister renounces Smith. When Smith's son, visiting from the North, learns of the preacher's hypocrisy, he leaves his mother's home. The play ends with Smith's admission that she crossed Aunt Dinah and thereby brought about the misfortune of her son's leaving and the minister's ire. In *A Stranger from Beyond*, an unknown man appears at a remote rural home. Through roots and herbs, he cures the dying mother of Sam, Sis, and Bud, telling them that he "helps those who can't help theirselves [*sic*]." He leaves as mysteriously as he had arrived. *Near Calvary* retells the story of Simon the Cyrenian, who carried the cross for Jesus. In *The Holy Spirit*, set on the eve of the Nativity, the spirits of Love, Faith, Joy, and Brotherhood visit Mary and Joseph to tell them of the gifts Jesus will bring to mankind. In *Man of Magic*, a visitor doubts the magical powers of a wealthy and generous king. Afriarmi, the king, reveals to the man that he, the king, is of a new race, one neither black nor white. Through love, he explains, this power is available to all people.

Richardson wrote six essays on African-American drama. Published in *Crisis*, *Opportunity*, and *The Messenger*, the leading black magazines of the period, Richardson's essays provided the strongest black voice, outside of theater critic Theophilus Lewis and Du Bois, in calling for a black national theater. In his essays, Richardson complained about the state of black drama as he cajoled his readers to support the theater and advised them of its value as an educational medium. The only body of theory written on black drama by the 1920s, Richardson's essays laid out what he saw as the purpose of black drama. His first essay, "The Hope of Negro Drama," which appeared in *Crisis* in November 1919, was published shortly before *The Deacon's Awakening*, his first play. The essay is a plea for the development of "Negro drama" that "shows the soul of a people." He writes of creating plays drawn from the lives of "porters, cooks, and waiters" ("Hope" 338). In his second essay, "The Negro and the Stage," which was published in *Opportunity* in October 1924, Richardson points out that no theaters exist "where Negro actors play in plays whose themes are particularly Negro" (310). "To see the Negro on stage," he notes, "has been to laugh." Richardson hoped for the development of black actors and theaters that would address African-American life as whites were unable to do.

In his third essay "Propaganda in the Theatre," which was published in *The Messenger* in November 1924, Richardson urges that the stage be used "for the purpose of changing the opinions of people" (353). Through educational plays, he wrote, "wonders may be done for the cause of the Negro," adding that "every phase and condition of life may be depicted." In this essay, Richardson pointed out that dialect should evoke pride, rather than shame, among African Americans for it was the "mother tongue of the American Negro" (354).

Richardson's other three essays appeared in *Opportunity* during 1925. In "Characters," he cautions against what were called "best foot forward plays," that is, plays that depicted blacks in only a positive manner. In "The Negro Audience," Richardson noted that black audiences were generally uneducated about the theater, expecting only to laugh and be entertained. He complained also of the lack of attendance by blacks at serious theater productions, claiming that the audience was partly responsible for the success or failure of black drama. "A Negro," he wrote, "seldom . . . hear[s] a Negro play with an open mind. [He] thinks the Negro should be portrayed as an angel." Richardson felt, "If Negro drama is to prosper, the Negro [audience] must learn . . . whether the characters are well-drawn, whether the dialogue is natural, whether the ending is consistent and whether the whole thing is interesting and logical" (123). In his final essay, "The Unpleasant Play," Richardson returned to his ongoing complaint about the flatness of characters in plays by blacks, again noting that black audiences seemed to want only happy endings or triumphant black characters rather than life as it really was.

In addition to his interest in drama, Richardson worked on short stories and poetry. Although he had planned to write twelve stories, only seven were completed before his death in 1977. Tentatively entitled *The Banny Simms Stories*, three stories feature the title character: "The Girl Hunter," "Mamie's Big Lie," and "The Trip across the Bridge." The four other stories that have been located—"The Teacher Dances," "The Midnight Ride to Winchester," "End of a Dropout," and "Indian Summer Event"—are highly autobiographical. Several of them are, in fact, pulled almost word for word from his unpublished autobiography. Relying on predictable plots and thin, anticlimactic story lines, the stories make evident that Richardson's strength in writing lay in writing plays rather than fiction.

The unpublished manuscript of 64 poems, entitled "Victorian Poems," is located in the Schomburg Center for Research in Black Culture in Harlem. This writer has seen only one published poem by Richardson; "The After-Thought" appeared in *Crisis* in June 1923:

> Oh that last night I said I did not care,
> But I was fretful from an angry sting;

And in my petulance was unaware
Of what great change a few hours' thought would bring.

Now you are gone, my days are bleak and long
And vacant as a sail-deserted sea;
Silent is my poor heart's divinest song,
Dead all those dreams of hope that lived in me.

Richardson's poems are highly suggestive of Alfred Lord Tennyson, a British poet popular in the late nineteenth century and one
whose poems appear to have also influenced Angelina Grimké,
who provided critiques for several of Richardson's poems. As Cornelius Weygandt has pointed out, "Americans all over the country
heard Tennyson from the pulpit" and that "his verses were on
Christmas cards and calendars and in the poet's corner in newspapers and in the almanacs." His poetry would, no doubt, have been
widely read by those who sought middle-class, or genteel, bear-
ings, for Tennyson's treasured poetry was "for fifty years a parlor-
table book in America" (Weygandt 109).[3]

The poems, written in a regular meter and rhyme, frequently al-
lude to figures from Greek and Roman mythology. Richardson
wrote poems on the deaths of Lincoln and black composer Samuel
Coleridge-Taylor. Matters of racial conflict and skin color are not
mentioned; instead, the poems seem very personal, their topics
centering usually on lost love, missed dreams, and loneliness. Indeed, with their tone of regret and solitude, the poems seem to be
Richardson's assessment of his own life.

NOTES

1. Richardson commented on this in his papers, writing, "I put in
some [plays] of mine and some of May Miller's. Miller's father [Kelly
Miller, a dean at Howard] told her that she shouldn't allow her plays to
be in the book unless her name was on the cover. I didn't mind her name
being on the cover, and so that's how the book happens to be by both of
us" (Unpublished notes).

2. In 1922, Woodson wrote that blacks "must learn to tell the story
ourselves." He argued that African Americans "should develop a literature . . . and read things written by their own people" See "Some Things
Negroes Need to Do." *Southern Workman* 51 (1922): 34. In 1931, Woodson
noted, "Negroes studying dramatics now go into our schools to repro-

duce Shakespeare, but mentally developed members of this race would see the possibilities of a greater drama in the tragedy of the man of color" See *The Miseducation of the Negro*. Washington, D.C. Associated Publishers, 1933: 140.

3. In *Tennyson in America*, John O. Eidson notes that "It was the four *Idylls of the King* published in 1859 that opened to [Tennyson] the heart of the public and began that immense popularity which [Tennyson] never saw diminished" (148). At his death in 1892, Tennyson and his Arthurian poem were still tremendously popular in America. The wide-spread popularity of Tennyson in the late nineteenth and early twentieth centuries suggests that it is highly probable that as a student Grimké studied Tennyson's poetry while she attended elite private schools in the North. More than likely she also taught his poetry in her English classes at the M Street School, which Richardson attended.

Afterword

"Never let a nigger say a line" was, according to Sterling Brown, an "old theatrical commandment" from white stage veterans in the early twentieth century; it was their belief that blacks on stage should be confined to song and dance routines. From 1890 to 1920, African Americans on stage obeyed this rule; rarely speaking straight lines, they, instead, crooned and joked, most often as comedians, dancers, and singers—all perpetuating the image of the uninhibited black. Behind this facade, however, lay the quotidian reality of most African-American men and women.

The actual lives led by most African Americans were much different from the grinning masks worn and the ebullience displayed on stage. The elevator operator at the Waldorf Astoria, the black laundress in a white household, the student trying to find materials on black history, the grandparents left behind in the South when the family bundled grandchildren and Bibles and moved to Detroit or Chicago for factory jobs, the African-American soldier who fought in Europe defending a country that was still lynching his brothers, the families undergoing stress and separation as they adjusted to life in urban areas—these Americans had lives quite different from those depicted on the boards in musical productions. And it is these American citizens and their lives that the early

African-American dramatists acknowledge and enact on simple stages. In American society in general, the experiences of these African Americans received little notice. Consequently, these "invisible people" had no voice in the theater or really in any major aspect of American life outside of their communities.

Bert Williams became possibly the most popular black vaudeville entertainer of the early twentieth century through his role as the "poor, shunted, cheated, out-of-luck Negro" (Fauset 12). Although Williams was said to have "unlocked the doors of the American theater to later Negro artists," some black writers thought that Williams had sold out by presenting and thereby promoting the image of the inferior black, a popular and financially successful image in white theaters (Gregory, "Drama" 156). To many blacks, Williams had become successful in the white world by selling out his culture. According to one critic, Williams's was the "ignoble lot of dragging his people through the flotsam and jetsam of art to the derisive and vulgar hand-clapping of race-prejudiced America" ("Bert Williams" 394). Aware of the ambiguity of his position, Williams often spoke of hearing the applause for his performance as he rode the freight elevator down to leave by the service exit. In his only essay, Williams wrote, "I have never been able to discover anything disgraceful in being a colored man. But I have often found it inconvenient—in America" (6).

The African-American playwrights of the 1920s did not dismiss all elements of the minstrel and vaudeville stages. They capitalized on some of them, keeping dialect in several instances, occasionally portraying characters as superstitious, ignorant, or poor. But in the plays of the pioneer dramatists the tone changed. In the plays written for the black non-musical stage during its formative years, black characters acquired a dignity that had not been accorded them previously. Prior to the plays of the late teens, 1917–1919, no playwright—black or white, European or American—had put on stage an accurate depiction of African-American life, one interpreted by blacks, one written for blacks. The pioneering black playwrights of the numerous little-theater groups did this, and they did so by creating a form of theater free of stereotypes, formulas, and clichés; they constructed a stage for black voices speaking black works written for black people.

The folk drama, a form that Du Bois had praised, provided Richardson and other black dramatists with a freedom they hadn't had, for this form of drama sprang from a past with which both African-American playwrights and their audiences were familiar. It gave the dramatists a venue for presenting topics to which African-American audiences could relate, topics that portrayed life as many of them had indeed experienced it. Through the medium of the folk play, writers created plots in rural settings with stories centered on family tensions, poverty, miscegenation, and lynching. The characters and situations were drawn from the lower class, the "simple folk"; rather than deny his folk heritage, Willis Richardson, among many other early African-American playwrights, embraced it.

It has been said that in English departments "American drama [is] an unwanted bastard child" (Smith 112). Should plays be read or acted? Perhaps drama should be taught in theater courses? How can American drama possibly compete with that of, for instance, the British tradition? If American drama is indeed a "bastard child," then dramatic works by African Americans, especially the plays before 1930, are orphans, for these playwrights were without parents in that they had no suitable stage traditions or mentors to guide and support them.

Although there had been models, so to speak, on the black stage, these were simply no longer sufficient or satisfactory for a race that was trying to throw off the shackles of the nineteenth century and what it stood for in the minds of black Americans. The African-American playwrights did have ancestors, but their works did not offer the changed image that the black playwrights, and many African Americans, wanted in the new century. The black playwrights of the early twentieth century wanted different images of African Americans on their stages. Previous representations of blacks, the ones that embarrassed them, those that held back the race through their reinforcement of the comic or tragic darkey, those who used white plays as their models, were neither adequate nor accurate.

Creating a voice for and real-izing—that is, making real—black versions of the African-American tale were the goals of the many men and women who wrote plays in the early part of this century. Mary Burrill, Georgia Johnson, and May Miller, to name a few, could be called true stage mothers in that these women "birthed" the black theater tradition. Richardson, Randolph Edmonds, John Matheus, and other male playwrights might be considered the fathers, as they, too, joined in creating a black theater that was "for us, about us, by us and near us." Through their dramas, the black playwrights of the twenties, like Hansberry's Younger family in a Chicago ghetto, sought to "disobey the massa" and build a drama around the experiences found in African-American life.

Attempting to revive interest in the work of Willis Richardson has not been simple. Many questions that I sought to answer I had to let go: Who were his parents? I never could locate a copy of his play *The Conjure Man Dies*, although its title fascinated me. I was not able to satisfy myself about the extent to which Richardson's background was searched in relation to suspected Communist activities in the 1930s and 1940s. Nor have I been able to complete the production records of his plays. Some answers will no doubt surface; some areas will, however, always remain murky. Such gaps, frustrations, and challenges are found in much primary research, I understand.

Rather than be nagged by these and many other questions, I find that I have some sense of satisfaction in having delved into Richardson's life and work to a greater extent than has been done. Through my research, I have become convinced of the necessity of recovering his plays and essays on drama. More than ever, I believe that his work must be considered in recounting the history of American drama. Perhaps this book has led others to this same belief. Perhaps it will add one tile to the mosaic of this picture.

In researching this topic over the past six years, I have come across several books on African-American female playwrights. In *Their Place on the Stage* (1988), Elizabeth Brown-Guillory surveys the history of African-American female dramatists. Her *Wines in the Wilderness* (1991) anthologizes several early plays, as does Kathy Perkins's *Black Female Playwrights before 1950* (1989). Plays by Angelina Grimké, Georgia Johnson, Mary Burrill, and May Miller stand next to works by Adrienne Kennedy and Alice Childress in these collections as being worthy of recognition in this field. I have also attended countless lectures, panels, and papers on African-American women who were writing plays during the New Negro Renaissance. Written by black American women, lynching plays, kitchen table plays, and mother-daughter plays are now being included in university courses in Women's Studies, African-American literature, and American drama. Attendant commentaries on plays by black women have been, over the past five years, much easier to locate in scholarly journals. Such recovery work and acknowledgments indicate early black playwrights are finally being recovered, preserved through publication, and studied.

I am troubled, however, by the lack of scholarship on plays by African-American male playwrights before 1930. When I have mentioned this lack, colleagues have answered that male playwrights "are published more often and receive more attention in research journals." In pursuing this response, however, I have found only a handful of people who are able to name one African-American male playwright of the 1920s other than Jean Toomer and his play *Kabnis*. This chasm, this lack of awareness, explains my dedication to research on plays written by African-American men before and during the 1920s. As I have attempted to show in this book, several men were writing plays and their plays differ in striking ways from those by women.

Much remains to be done in this entire field—-regardless of the gender of the playwright. This book is meant as a start, perhaps as a signal, that this area waits—as it has for decades—for someone to go through boxes on back shelves in library basements, to open dusty files, and to begin reading. Most African-American little-theater groups throughout the United States have a history still to be recounted. No doubt now-elderly African Americans have yellowed scripts from the plays or sat in those early audiences. Assembling the history of the early African-American little theater will not be done by only searching the archives of universities; only one part of the story lies there.

At the outset of this study, I, as did many of my colleagues, believed that only a few plays had been written by black Americans and those by only a few playwrights. For the most part, I had thought that African Americans involved in theater were found only on the musical stage. I learned otherwise when I first opened *Crisis* magazine and found an unassuming essay entitled "The Hope of a Negro Drama," by a man named Willis Richardson. Thus far, over 115 African Americans have been identified as having written before 1930 over 350 plays for the African-American non-musical stage. These numbers alone raise questions: why, we might ask, is so little known of these plays and their writers? What do these plays reveal about aspects of African-American art and culture that were not controlled by whites? How can a background in American drama be possible without an awareness of these early contributions?

Through this study, some modicum of attention has been given to a neglected part of American drama. Perhaps in becoming aware of the work of the early playwrights, we are able to piece together the traditions seen on today's black stage. But more than this, we are given a much fuller, a more accurate, picture of American drama. In acknowledging the works of Richardson and his contemporaries, we as readers are able to question not only the canon of American drama but also that very term. Perhaps an increased awareness of these early playwrights will lead toward making American drama truly that—American drama rather than white drama.

In reading African-American plays written before 1930, or those of any period before *A Raisin in the Sun* (1959), a new dimension is opened to us. For the plays reveal African-American concerns and methods of simple and daily survival more immediately, more freshly, than materials written by today's theater historians. These plays are primary documents in the truest sense in that they were written to be performed and not necessarily published. Even if one does not see merit in the individual plays, it is difficult for a reader, once familiar with the number and the content of these works, to return to current American plays with the same perspective—whether those plays are by Miller, Williams, and O'Neill, or by Baraka, Ntozake Shange, and August Wilson. For having read these early plays, we know both that there are many other voices in American drama and the roots from which these later black playwrights drew. By our becoming aware of these overlooked plays, we not only take a step in their recovery through our acknowledgment, but we also are able to speak, read, and write about American drama, indeed, American literature, in a more informed manner.

More than any other African-American dramatist, Richardson contributed to the development of African-American drama during the 1920s. His plays are important for their portrayals of life as many African Americans dealt with it. The characters are, as he wanted them to be, ordinary. The plots are not filled with high drama or emotion. But it is in this regard that they are distinctive, for his stage reveals African-American life as many, no doubt, experienced it. His plays are, quite obviously, in a whole other category than the works associated with the "Harlem Renaissance." This is, perhaps, their distinguishing feature, for they reveal black lives apart from those "owned and operated" by white readers, spectators, reviewers, and publishers.

In reviewing only these few plays, we might ask why folk plays in general and Richardson's in particular are not better known. So many elements of the African-American tradition are found in them. In content, Richardson's plays, for example, are set in the black community, and their focus is for the most part on the folk. In form, his plays and those by other black playwrights writing for little theaters are community events and are, obviously, part of an oral tradition. More than this, the plays for and by African-American community groups were also about them and affirmations of them. Through folk drama, African Americans *un*covered a voice for themselves and *dis*covered a fresh voice for the American stage, a voice that was not confounded by a European aesthetic, but a form that spoke *about* and *to* African Americans. To a great degree, this definition and development, this advocacy for an African-American voice, came about through the pen of Willis Richardson.

Plays by Willis Richardson

The following plays are identified as having been written by Richardson. Those marked with an asterisk have been published.

The Amateur Prostitute (192?)

*Antonio Maceo (1932?)

Attucks, the Martyr (192?) (Also entitled *Crispus Attucks* and *A Killing in Boston*)

*The Black Horseman (1935)

The Bold Lover (192?)

*The Bootblack Lover (1926)

*The Broken Banjo (1925)

The Brown Boy (192?)

The Chasm (with E. C. Williams) (1926)

*The Children's Treasure (1921)

*The Chip Woman's Fortune (1923)

*Compromise (1925)

The Curse of the Shell-Road Witch (192?)

The Dark Haven (192?)

*The Deacon's Awakening (1921)

The Dope King (192?)

The Dragon's Tooth (1921)

The Elder Dumas (192?)

The Fall of the Conjurer (1925)

Family Discord (192?)

Fight for Freedom (193?)

The Flight of the Natives (1927)

Gaspard, the Oppressor (192?)

The Gypsy's Finger-Ring (1921)

The Holy Spirit: A Playlet (192?)

Hope of the Lowly: A Play in Three Acts (192?)

The House of Sham (1929)

The Idle Head (1929)

Imp of the Devil (192?)

In Menelik's Court (192?)

Invitation to a Duel (193?)

The Jail Bird (192?)

Joy Rider (192?)

The King's Dilemma (1920)

Man of Magic (192?)

The Man who Married a Young Wife (192?)

Miss or Mrs.: A Comedy (1941)

Mortgaged (1924)

Near Calvary (193?)

The New Generation (192?)

The New Lodgers (192?)

The Nude Siren: A Farce (192?)

The Peacock's Feathers (192?)

A Pillar of the Church (192?)

Rooms for Rent (1926)

Sacrifice (1930)

A Stranger from Beyond (192?)

Victims (192?) (originally titled The Deep Regret)

The Visiting Lady (192?)

The Wine Seller (1927)

Bibliography

Abrahamson, Doris E. *Negro Playwrights in the American Theatre 1925–1959.* New York: Columbia UP, 1969.

Anderson, George C. "The Negro and the Stage." In *The Voice of the Negro.* [1919] Ed. Robert Kerlin. New York: Arno, 1968. 166–67.

Anderson, Jervis. "Our Far-Flung Correspondents: A Very Special Monument." *New Yorker* 20 Mar. 1978: 93+.

Austin, Patricia Addell. "Pioneering Black Authored Dramas: 1924–1927." Diss. Michigan State U, 1986.

Baker, Houston. *Modernism and the Harlem Renaissance.* Chicago: U of Chicago P, 1987.

"Beginnings of a Negro Drama." *Literary Digest* 48 (1914): 1114.

Belcher, Fannin S. Jr. "The Place of the Negro in the Evaluation of the American Theatre, 1767–1940." Diss. Yale U, 1945.

Bernardine, Brother. Letter to Willis Richardson. 23 May 1937. Willis Richardson Papers. Billy Rose Collection. New York Public Library at Lincoln Center, New York. (Hereafter referred to as WRP, BRC, NYPL, LC.).

———. Letter to Willis Richardson. 8 Aug. 1937. WRP, BRC, NYPL, LC.

Bernstein, Richard. "August Wilson's Voices from the Past." *New York Times* 27 Mar. 1988: H-34.

"Bert Williams." *The Messenger* 4 (Apr. 1922): 394.

Bigsby, C.W.E. *The Second Black Renaissance: Essays in Black Literature.* Westport, CT: Greenwood Press, 1980.

Birmingham, Stephen. *Certain People: America's Black Elite*. Boston: Little, Brown, 1977.

Bond, Frederick W. *The Negro and the Drama* [1940]. College Park, MD: McGrath, 1969.

Bone, Robert. Down Home: *A History of Afro-American Short Fiction from Its Beginning to the End of the Harlem Renaissance*. New York: Putnam, 1975.

―――. *The Negro Novel in America*. Rev. ed. New Haven: Yale UP, 1965.

Bontemps, Arna. "The Awakening: A Memoir." In *The Harlem Renaissance Remembered: Essays Edited with a Memoir*. Ed. Arna Bontemps. New York: Dodd, Mead, 1972. 1–26.

Boskin, Joseph. *Sambo: The Rise and Demise of an American Jester*. New York: Oxford UP, 1986.

Braithwaite, William Stanley. "The Negro in Literature." *Crisis* (1924): 204–10.

Branch, Williams S., ed. *Crosswinds: An Anthology of Black Dramatists in the Diaspora*. Bloomington: Indiana UP, 1993.

Brown, Sterling A. "Concerning Negro Drama." *Opportunity* 9 (1931): 284+.

―――. "Negro Character as Seen by White Authors." *Journal of Negro Education* 2 (1933): 179–203.

―――. *Negro Poetry and Drama and the Negro in American Fiction*. Washington, D.C.: Association in Negro Folk Education, 1937.

―――, et al., eds. *The Negro Caravan* [1941]. New York: Arno Press, 1969.

Brown-Guillory, Elizabeth, ed. *Their Place on the Stage: Black Women Playwrights in America*. New York: Praeger, 1988.

―――. ed. *Wines in the Wilderness: Plays by African American Women from the Harlem Renaissance to the Present*. New York: Praeger, 1990.

Bruce, Dickson D., Jr. *Black Writing from the Nadir: The Evolution of a Literary Tradition 1877–1915*. Baton Rouge: Louisiana State UP, 1989.

Brunvand, Jan Harold. *The Study of American Folklore: An Introduction*. 2nd ed. New York: Norton, 1978.

Busia, Abena P. B. "Words Whispered over Voids: A Context for Black Women's Rebellious Voices in the Novel of the African Diaspora." *Studies in Black American Literature*. 3 (1988): 1–41.

By River, by Rail: The Great Migration North. Narr. Maya Angelou. CBS. WBAL, Baltimore. 28 Dec. 1994.

Clarke, John Henrik. "The Neglected Dimensions of the Harlem Renaissance." *Black World* 20 (Nov. 1920): 118–29.

Clum, John. "Ridgely Torrence's Negro Plays." *South Atlantic Quarterly* 68 (1969): 96–108.

Cogdell, Josephine. "Truth in Art in America." *The Messenger* 5 (Apr. 1923): 634–36.

Coleman, Edwin Leon, Jr. "Langston Hughes: An American Dramatist."
    Diss. U of Oregon, 1971.
———. "Carl Van Vechten Presents the New Negro." In Kramer 1987.
    107–27.
Coleman, Mike. "What Is Black Theater?: An Interview with Imamu
    Amiri Baraka." *Black World* 20 (Apr. 1971): 32–38.
"The Contest." *Opportunity* 3 (1925): 130–31.
Cooley, John. "In Pursuit of the Primitive: Black Portraits by Eugene
    O'Neill and Other Village Bohemians" In Kramer 1987. 51–64.
Cooper, Anna Julia. Postcard to Alain Locke. Alain Locke Papers. Coll.
    164: Box 21: Folder 53. Moorland Spingarn Research Center,
    Manuscript Division. Howard University. Washington, D.C.
    (Hereafter referred to as ALP, MSRC, MD, HU.).
Cruse, Harold. *The Crisis of the Negro Intellectual: A Historical Analysis of the
    Failure of Black Leadership*. New York: Quill, 1984.
Cullen, Countee. "The Dark Tower." *Opportunity* 5 (1927): 180–81.
Daniel, Walter C. Black Journals of the United States. Westport, CT:
    Greenwood Press, 1982.
———. "Du Bois's First Efforts as a Playwright." *CLAJ* 33 (1990): 418–30.
Davis, Allison. "Our Negro 'Intellectuals.' " *Crisis* (1928): 268+.
Davis, Arthur P. *From the Dark Tower: Afro-American Writers 1900–1960*.
    Washington, D.C.: Howard UP,1974.
———. Letter to the author. 24 June 1993.
Davis, Arthur P., and Michael Peplow, eds. *The New Negro Renaissance*.
    New York: Holt, Winston and Rinehart, 1975.
De Armond, Fred. "A Note on the Sociology of Negro Literature." *Oppor-
    tunity* 3 (1925): 369–71.
Didier, Rogier. Review of "Dixie to Broadway." *Opportunity* 2 (1924): 345–46.
Dixon, Melvin. "The Rusty Aesthetic." *Black World* 20 (May 1971): 40–46.
Du Bois, W.E.B. *The Autobiography of W.E.B. Du Bois* New York: Interna-
    tional Publishers, 1968.
———. "Can the Negro Serve the Drama?" *Theatre* 38 (1923) 12+.
———. "Criteria of Negro Art." *Crisis* (1926): 290–97.
———. "The Drama among Black Folk." *Crisis* (1916): 169+.
———. *The Dusk of Dawn: An Essay Toward an Autobiography of a Race Con-
    cept*. [1940] New Brunswick: Transaction Publishers, 1992.
———. "Krigwa, 1926." *Crisis* (1926): 115.
———. "Krigwa Players Little Negro Theater." *Crisis* (1926): 134–36.
———. Letter to Alain Locke. 14 May 1927. Coll. 164: Box 26: Folder 8.
    ALP, MSRC, MD, HU.
———. "The National Emancipation Exposition." *Crisis* (1913): 339–41.
———. "The Negro and the American Stage." *Crisis* (1924): 6–57.

————. "Negro Art." *Crisis* (1921): 55–56.

————. "A Negro Art Renaissance." *Los Angeles Times* 14 June 1925: pt. 3, 26–27.

————. "A Pageant." *Crisis* (1915): 230–31.

————. "Paying for Plays." *Crisis* (1926): 7–8.

————. "The Social Origins of American Negro Art." *Modern Quarterly* 3 (1925): 53–56.

————. *The Souls of Black Folk* [1903]. New York: Penguin, 1989.

————. "The Star of Ethiopia." *Crisis* (1915): 90–93.

Dunbar, Paul Laurence. "We Wear the Mask." [1895] In *Black Writers of America: A Comprehensive Anthology*. Richard Barksdale and Keneth Kinnamon, eds. New York: Macmillan, 1972. 352.

Early, Gerald, ed. *Speech and Power*. 2 vols. Hopewell, NJ: Ecco, 1993.

Edmonds, Randolph. "Black Drama in the American Theatre: 1700–1970." In *The American Theatre: A Sum of Its Parts*. New York: French, 1971. 379–426.

————. Review of "Negro Play Number" (*Carolina Magazine*, ed. by Frederick Koch). *Opportunity* 7 (1929): 318.

Eidson, John Olin. *Tennyson in America: His Reputation and Influence from 1827 to 1858*. Athens, GA: U of Georgia P, 1943.

Ellison, Ralph. "The Art of Fiction." Interview in *Shadow and Act*. New York: Random House, 1964. 167–83.

————. "The World and The Jug." In *Shadow and Act*. New York: Random House, 1964. 107–43.

Farrison, William Edward. *William Wells Brown: Author and Reformer*. Chicago: U of Chicago P, 1969.

Fauset, Jessie. "The Symbolism of Bert Williams." *Crisis* (1922): 12–14.

Fehrenbach, Robert. "Angelina Grimké's Rachel." In *Wild Women in the Whirlwind: Afra-American Culture and the Contemporary Literary Renaissance*. Ed. Joanne Braxton and Andree Nicola McLaughlin. New Brunswick, NJ: Rutgers UP, 1990. 88–106.

Flynn, Joyce. "Melting Plots: Patterns of Racial and Ethnic Amalgamation in American Drama before Eugene O'Neill." *American Quarterly* 38 (1986): 417–38.

Forrest, Marie Moore. "Notes." In Thomas Montgomery Gregory Papers. Coll. 37: Box 3: Folder 92. (Hereafter referred to as TMGP MSRC, MD, HU.).

Fort-Whiteman, Lovett. "Drama." *The Messenger* 5 (1923): 671.

Gatewood, Willard B. *Aristocrats of Color: The Black Elite, 1880–1920*. Bloomington: Indiana UP, 1990.

"The Gilpin Players of Cleveland." *Crisis* (1930): 191+.

Goggin, Jacqueline. *Carter G. Woodson: A Life in Black History*. Baton Rouge: Louisiana State UP, 1993.

Green, Elizabeth Lay. *The Negro in Contemporary American Literature* [1928]. College Park, MD: McGrath, 1968.

Gregory, Thomas Montgomery. "A Chronology of the Negro Theatre." In *Plays of Negro Life*. Ed. Alain Locke [1927]. Westport, CT: Negro UP, 1968. 409–23.

———. "The Drama of Negro Life." In *The New Negro* [1925]. New York: Atheneum, 1970. 53–67.

———. Letter to Willis Richardson. 28 Apr. 1940. Richardson Family.

———. "Negro Drama." Typescript. Re: Howard Players. Coll. 37: Box 3: Folder 92. TMGP MSRC, MD, HU.

———. Review of *The No 'Count Boy* by Paul Green. *Opportunity* 3 (1925): 121–22.

Griffin, George W. H. *Hamlet the Dainty: An Ethiopian Burlesque on Shakespeare's* Hamlet. The Ethiopian Drama, no. 49. New York: Happy Hours, 1870.

Grimké, Angelina. "*Rachel*: The Play of the Month." *Competitor* 1 (1920): 51–52.

Hall, Jean Richardson. Letter to the author. 25 Jan. 1992.

———. Personal interview. 17 Mar. 1992.

Halton, Ernest. Phone interview. 10 Mar. 1992.

Hamalian, Leo, and James V. Hatch, eds. *The Lost Plays of the Harlem Renaissance, 1920–1940*. Detroit: Wayne State UP, 1996.

———. *The Roots of African-American Drama: An Anthology of Early Plays, 1858–1938*. Detroit: Wayne State UP, 1991.

Harrington, John P. Preface. *Modern Irish Drama*. New York: Norton, 1991. viii–xiv.

Hartt, Rollin Lynde. "The Negro in Drama." *Crisis* (1922): 61–64.

Hatch, James V., and Ted Shine, eds. *Black Theater, U.S.A.: Forty-Five Plays by Black Americans: 1847–1974*. New York: Free Press, 1974.

Hatch, James V. Letter to the author. 6 Oct. 1992.

———. "A White Folks' Guide to Two Hundred Years of Black and White Drama." *Drama Review* 16 (1972): 4–24.

Hay, Samuel A. *African American Theatre: An Historical and Critical Analysis*. New York: Cambridge UP, 1994.

Hopkins, Pauline Elizabeth. *Peculiar Sam, or The Underground Railroad*. In *The Roots of African-American Drama*. Ed. Leo Hamalian and James V. Hatch. Detroit: Wayne State UP, 1991. 96–123.

Huggins, Nathan Irvin. *Harlem Renaissance*. New York: Oxford UP, 1971.

Hughes, Langston. *The Big Sea*. New York: Hill and Wang, 1940.

———. "Our Wonderful Society: Washington." *Opportunity* 5 (1927): 226–27.

Hutchinson, George. *The Harlem Renaissance in Black and White*. Cambridge, MA: Belknap Press, 1995.

Hyman, Thelma. Letter to the author. 5 Jan. 1992.

Ikonne, Chidi. *From Du Bois to Van Vechten: The Early New Negro Literature, 1903–1926*. Westport, CT: Greenwood Press, 1981.

Isaacs, Edith. Review of *Plays of Negro Life. Opportunity* 6 (1927): 374.

Jackson, Wallace V. "The Negro Stage." *The Messenger* 5 (1923): 746–48.

Jelliffe, Rowena Woodham. "The Gilpin Players." *Opportunity* 6 (1928): 344–45.

———. Letter to Willis Richardson. 18 December 1951. WRP, BRC, NYPL, LC.

———. "The Negro in the Field of Drama." *Opportunity* 6 (1928): 214.

———. Personal interview. 1 Feb. 1992.

Jervay, Thomas. Letter to Willis Richardson. Richardson Family.

Johnson, Abby Arthur, and Ronald Mayberry Johnson. *Propaganda and Aesthetics: The Literary Politics of African American Magazines in the Twentieth Century*. Amherst: U of Massachusetts P, 1979.

Johnson, Charles S. "Rise of the Negro Magazine." *Journal of Negro History* 13 (Jan. 1928): 7–21.

Johnson, James Weldon. *Black Manhattan*. New York: Knopf, 1930.

———. "The Dilemma of the Negro Author." In Early, vol 1. 1993. 92–97.

———. Letter to Benjamin Brawley. 28 Nov. 1917. Benjamin G. Brawley Papers. Coll. 8: Box 1. MSRC, MD, HU.

Jones, LeRoi. *Blues People: Negro Music in White America*. New York: Morrow, 1963.

———. "The Revolutionary Theatre." *Home: Social Essays*. New York: Morrow, 1966. 210–15.

Kellner, Bruce, ed. *The Harlem Renaissance: A Historical Dictionary for the Era*. New York: Methuen, 1987.

———. " 'Refined Racism': White Patronage in the Harlem Renaissance." In Kramer 1987. 93–106.

Keyssar-Frank, Helene. *The Curtain and the Veil: Strategies in Black Drama*. New York: Burt Franklin, 1981.

King, Woodie, Jr., ed. *Black Theatre: Present Condition*. New York. National Black Theatre Touring Circuit, 1981.

———. Speech. National Conference of African American Theatre. Baltimore, 8 Apr. 1995.

———. Introduction. In his ed. *New Plays for the Black Theatre*. Chicago: Third World Press, 1989. i–v.

Kobor, Noemi. Letter to Willis Richardson. 11 Mar. 1931. WRP, BRC, NYPL, LC.

Koch, Frederick. Introduction. In his ed. *American Folk Plays*. New York: Appleton-Century, 1939. xiii–xxix.

Kornweibel, Theodore, Jr. *No Crystal Stair: Black Life and The Messenger, 1917–1928*. Westport, CT: Greenwood Press, 1975.

Kramer, Victor A., ed. *The Harlem Renaissance Re-examined*. New York: AMS Press, 1987.

Krasner, David. *Resistance, Parody, and Double Consciousness in African American Theatre, 1895–1910*. New York: St. Martin's Press, 1997.

Lewis, David Levering. *W.E.B. Du Bois: Biography of a Race, 1868–1919*. New York: Holt, 1993.

Locke, Alain. Drama Notes. Coll. 164: Box 27: Folder 27. ALP, MSRC, MD, HU.

———. "Introduction: The Drama of Negro Life." In *Plays of Negro Life: A Source-Book of Native American Drama*. Ed. Alain Locke [1927]. New York: Negro UP, 1968. xiii–xviii.

———. "The Legacy of the Ancestral Arts." In *The New Negro*. Ed. Alain Locke [1925]. New York: Atheneum, 1970. 254–67.

———. Letter to Montgomery Gregory. 15 Apr. 1929. Coll. 37: Box 2: Folder 52. TMGP, MSRC, MD, HU.

———. "Max Rheinhardt [*sic*] Reads the Negro's Dramatic Horoscope." *Opportunity* 2 (1924): 145–46.

———. "The Negro and the American Stage." *Theatre Arts Monthly* 10 (1926): 112–20.

———. "Steps toward the Negro Theatre." *Crisis* (1922): 66–68.

———. "1928: A Retrospective Review." *Opportunity* 7 (1929): 8–11.

Logan, Rayford W. *Howard University: The First Hundred Years 1867–1967*. New York: New York UP, 1969.

———. "Carter Godwin Woodson." In *Dictionary of American Negro Biography*. Ed. Rayford W. Logan and Michael Winston. New York: Norton, 1982: 665–67.

Lott, Eric. *Love and Theft: Blackface Minstrelsy and the American Working Class*. New York: Oxford UP, 1993.

Lowery, Charles D., and John F. Marszalek, eds. *Encyclopedia of African American Civil Rights: From Emancipation to the Present*. Westport, CT: Greenwood Press, 1992.

Mackay, Constance D'Arcy. *The Little Theatre in the United States*. New York: Holt, 1917.

Martin, Tony. *Literary Garveyism: Garvey, Black Arts and the Harlem Renaissance*. Dover, MA: Majority Press, 1983.

Matthews, Brander. "The Rise and Fall of Negro Minstrelsy." *Scribner's* 57 (1915): 754–759.

McKay, Nellie. " 'What Were They Saying?': Black Women Playwrights of the Harlem Renaissance." In Kramer, 1987. 129–47.

McKelly, James C. "Hymns of Sedition: Portraits of the Artist in Contemporary African American Drama." *Arizona Quarterly* 48 (1992): 87–107.

McKinney, Ernest Rice. "*Rachel*: A Play by Angelina W. Grimké." *Competitor* 1 (1920): 35–36.

Meier, August, and Elliott Rudwick. *Black History and the Historical Profession 1915–1980*. Urbana: U of Illinois P, 1986.

———. *From Plantation to Ghetto*. 3rd ed. New York: Hill and Wang, 1976.

Molette, Barbara J. Personal interview. 8 Apr. 1995.

Molette, Carlton W., and Barbara J. Molette. *Black Theater: Premise and Presentation*. Bristol, IN: Wyndham Hall, 1985.

Moses, Montrose. *The American Dramatist*. New York: Blom, 1925.

Moses, Wilson Jeremiah. *Black Messiahs and Uncle Toms: Social and Literary Manipulations of a Religious Myth*. Rev. ed. University Park: Pennsylvania. State UP, 1993.

Nathan, George Jean. "The Black Art." In *Mr. George Jean Nathan Presents*. New York: Knopf, 1917. 115–21.

O'Dell, George C. D. "The Negro Theatre, 1821–1922." *Annals of the New York Stage*. Vol. 3. New York: Columbia UP, 1927. 34–37.

———. "The Padlock." *Annals of the New York Stage*. Vol. 1. New York: Columbia UP, 1927. 151.

Office of Personnel Management. Employment Records of Willis Richardson. 1911– 1954. St. Louis.

"On the Need of Better Plays." *Opportunity* 5 (1927): 5–6.

"On Writing about Negroes." *Opportunity* 3 (1925): 227–28.

O'Neil, Raymond. "The Negro in Dramatic Art." *Crisis* (1924): 155–57.

O'Neill, Eugene. Letter in "Comments on the Negro Actor." *The Messenger* 7 (1925): 17–18.

———. Letter to Montgomery Gregory. 25 Jan. 1921. Coll. 37: Box 3: Folder 92. TMGP MSRC, MD, HU.

Otis, C. Letter. *Opportunity* 1 (1923): 283.

Pakenham, Thomas. *The Scramble for Africa: White Man's Conquest of the Dark Continent from 1867 to 1912*. New York: Avon, 1991.

Paskman, Gerald, and Sigmund Spaeth. *"Gentlemen, Be Seated!" A Parade of the Old-Time Minstrels*. Garden City, NY: Doubleday Doran, 1928.

Pawley, Thomas D. "The First Black Playwrights." *Black World* (Apr. 1972): 16–24.

Perkins, Kathy, ed. *Black Female Playwrights: An Anthology of Plays before 1950*. Bloomington: Indiana UP, 1989.

Perry, Shauneille. Keynote address. National Conference of African American Theatre. Baltimore, 7 April 1995.

Peterson, Bernard L., Jr. *A Century of Musicals in Black and White: An Encyclopedia of Musicals and Stage Works by, About, or Involving African Americans*. Westport, CT: Greenwood Press, 1993.

———. *Contemporary Black American Playwrights and Their Plays: A Biographical Directory and Dramatic Index*. Westport, CT: Greenwood Press, 1988.

———. *Early Black American Playwrights and Dramatic Writers: A Biographical Directory and Catalog of Plays, Films, and Broadcasting Scripts*. Westport, CT: Greenwood Press, 1990.

———. "Willis Richardson." *Black World* 26 no. 6 (April 1975): 41–48, 87–88.

Petesch, Donald A. *A Spy in the Enemy's Country: The Emergence of Modern Black Literature*. Iowa City: U of Iowa P, 1989.

Pierson, William D. *Black Legacy: America's Hidden Heritage*. Amherst: U of Massachusetts P, 1993.

Pieterse, Jan Nederveen. *White on Black: Images of Africa and Blacks in Western Popular Culture*. New Haven: Yale UP, 1992.

Prevots, Naima. *American Pageantry: A Movement for Art and Democracy*. Ann Arbor: UMI Research Press, 1990.

Quarles, Benjamin. *The Negro in the Making of America*. New York: Collier, 1964.

Revell, Peter. *Paul Laurence Dunbar*. Boston: Twayne, 1979.

Review of *Plays and Pageants from the Life of the Negro*. *Journal of Negro History* 15 (Apr. 1930): 263–64.

Riach, Douglas C. "Blacks and Blackface on the Irish Stage, 1830–60." *American Studies* 7 (1973): 231–42.

Rice, Naomi. Telephone interview. 3 Mar. 1992.

Richardson, Joyce. Letter to the author. 22 Jan. 1992.

———. Letter to the author. 10 Oct. 1993.

———. Personal interview. 14 Feb. 1992.

———. Personal interview. 17 Mar. 1992.

Richardson, Willis. "The After Thought." *Crisis* (1923): 58.

———. "Characters." *Opportunity* 3 (1925): 183.

———. "From Youth to Age." Autobiography. Typescript. Richardson Family.

———. "The Hope of a Negro Drama." *Crisis* 19 (1919): 338–39.

———. Introduction to *The Broken Banjo*. *Crisis* (1926): 167.

———. Introduction. *Plays and Pageants from the Life of the Negro.* Washington, D.C.: Associated Publishers, 1930. vii–x.

———. Letter to Alain Locke. 9 Aug. 1925. ALP, MSRC, MD, HU.

———. Letter to James V. Hatch. 7 Nov. 1972. Hatch-Billops Collection, New York City.

———. Letter to Montgomery Gregory. 13 Dec. 1922. TMGP, MSRC, MD, HU.

———. Letter to Thomas Jervay. Richardson Family.

———. "The Negro Audience." *Opportunity* 3 (1925): 123.

———. "The Negro and the Stage." *Opportunity* 2 (1924): 310.

———. Personal Notes. Richardson Family.

———. "The Play Prizes." Typescript. Richardson Family.

———. "Preface." *The Deacon's Awakening. Crisis* (1920): 167.

———. "Propaganda in the Theatre." *The Messenger* 6 (1924): 353–54.

———. Recorded interview with Cassandra Willis. Hatch-Billops Collection, New York City. 5 Mar. 1972.

———. Recorded interview with Larry Garvin. Hatch-Billops Collection, New York City. 27 July 1974.

———. "The Unpleasant Play." *Opportunity* 3 (1925): 282.

Rudwick, Elliott. *W.E.B. Du Bois: Propagandist of the Negro Protest.* Boston: Atheneum, 1968.

Sanders, Leslie Catherine. *The Development of Black Theater in America: From Shadows to Selves.* Baton Rouge: Louisiana State UP, 1988.

Selby, John. *Beyond Civil Rights.* Cleveland: World Publishing, 1966.

Seyboldt, Mark. "Play-Writing [*sic*]." *Crisis* (1925): 164–65.

Sinnette, Eleanor. "The Brownies' Book." *Freedomways* 5 (1965): 133–42.

Smith, Edward G. "Black Theatre." In *Ethnic Theatre in the United States.* Ed. Maxine Schwartz Seller. Westport, CT: Greenwood Press, 1983. 37–66.

"Something Else on the Stage." *Crisis* (1925): 39.

Spence, Eulalie. "A Criticism of the Negro Drama." *Opportunity* 6 (1928): 180.

———. "Negro Art Players in Harlem." *Opportunity* 6 (1928): 381.

Thomas, H. Nigel. *From Folklore to Fiction: A Study of Folk Heroes and Rituals in the Black American Novel.* Westport, CT: Greenwood Press, 1988.

Torrence, Ridgley. *Granny Maumee.* In *Plays of Negro Life: A Source-Book of Native American Drama.* Ed. Alain Locke [1927]. New York: Negro UP, 1968. 235–52.

Van Vechten, Carl. Letter. In "The Negro in Art: How Shall He Be Portrayed." *Crisis* (1926): 219.

————. "Uncle Tom's Mansion." In *Keep A-Inchin' Along: Selected Writings of Carl Van Vechten about Black Art and Letters*. Ed. Bruce Kellner. Westport, CT: Greenwood Press, 1979. 58–64.

Walrond, Eric. "The Theatre." *Opportunity* 2 (1924): 345–46.

"Washington and Virginia." *Crisis* (1929): 89–90.

Weygandt, Cornelius. *The Time of Tennyson: English Victorian Poetry as It Affected America*. Port Washington, NY: Kennicat, 1936.

White, Walter. "The Negro on the American Stage." *English Journal* 24 (1935): 179–88.

"Who Is Willis Richardson?" *The Journal* (Wilmington, NC) 8 May 1976: 1–2.

Williams, Allen. "Sheppard Randolph Edmonds: His Contributions to Black Educational Theatre." Diss. U of Indiana, 1972.

Williams, Bert. "The Comic Side of Trouble." In Early vol. 1. 3–9.

Wilson, August. "The Play." In *Joe Turner's Come and Gone*. New York: Plume, 1988. n.p.

Wittke, Carl. *Tambo and Bones: A History of the American Minstrel Stage*. Durham, NC: Duke UP, 1930.

Woll, Allen. *Black Musical Theatre: From Coontown to Dreamgirls*. Baton Rouge: Louisiana State UP, 1989.

Woodson, Carter G. "Celebration of Negro History Week." *Journal of Negro History* 12 (1927): 103–09.

————. Introduction. *Negro History in Thirteen Plays*. Ed. Willis Richardson and May Miller. Washington, D.C.: Associated Publishers, 1935. iii–v.

————. *The Miseducation of the Negro*. Washington, D.C.: Associated Publishers, 1933.

————. "Negro Life and History in Our Schools." *Journal of Negro History* 4 (1919): 273–80.

————. Review of *Negro History in Thirteen Plays*. *Journal of Negro History*. 21 (1936): 73–76.

————. "Some Things Negroes Need to Do." *Southern Workman* 51 (1922): 33–36.

Wright, Richard. "Blueprint for Negro Writing." In *Voices from the Harlem Renaissance* Ed. Nathan Irvin Huggins. New York: Oxford UP, 1995. 394–402.

Index

About the Author

CHRISTINE RAUCHFUSS GRAY is Assistant Professor of English at Catonsville Community College. She has contributed to the *Cambridge Companion to American Women Playwrights* (1997) and is the author of the critical introduction to the facsimile edition of *Plays and Pageants in the Life of the Negro* (1993).

Recent Titles in
Contributions in Afro-American and African Studies